A Parent's Guide to
Teaching Music

Jim Probasco

BETTERWAY PUBLICATIONS, INC.
WHITE HALL, VIRGINIA

Also by the same author:
A Parent's Guide to Band and Orchestra

Published by Betterway Publications, Inc.
P.O. Box 219
Crozet, VA 22932
(804) 823-5661

Cover photographs by Susan Riley
Typography by Park Lane Associates
Text illustrations by Mark Ashworth, Brent Probasco, and Dick
Probasco.

Library of Congress Cataloging-in-Publication Data
Probasco, Jim
    A parent's guide to teaching music / Jim Probasco.
      p. cm.
    Includes index.
    ISBN 1-55870-240-7 : $7.95
    1. Music—Instruction and study—Juvenile. I. Title.
  MT1.P765 1992
780'.7—dc20   91-43225
                                              CIP
                                                MN

Printed in the United States of America
0 9 8 7 6 5 4 3 2 1

*To Parent-Music Teachers Everywhere
And to David and Elaine Alexander,
Two of the best I know.*

ACKNOWLEDGMENTS

Many people have inspired me to want to learn about music.

There is my mother, Marion Probasco, of course. She bought me my first (and second) trombone and did it all while raising three children by herself and trying to put enough food on the table so my sister Sherry and I wouldn't have to eat our brother.

My mother-in-law, Nouna Taylor, quietly inspired me by making music such an important part of her life. Mom Taylor is the only person I've ever seen stop a lawn mower in the middle of the yard, run in the house, sit down, and start playing the piano for no apparent reason. Let's face it, you gotta admire *anyone* whose musical instincts are that strong!

When I was in high school, my friend, cousin, and former fifth grade teacher, Gary Hicks, broadened my musical (and culinary) horizons by taking me to New York and introducing me to Carnegie Hall, Lincoln Center, Broadway, and dinner at Mama Leone's, though not necessarily in that order.

And more recently, my GEnie parent-music teacher friends, Sherry, Linda, Sonsie, Liz, and Echo helped me keep my mind on my work by posing pertinent questions via computer modem. Questions such as:

What is the difference between Absolute Pitch and Perfect Pitch? (There's no difference.)

Is it true Suzuki students can't read music? (No.)

And my personal favorite: If you shine a flashlight in Madonna's left ear, how big a bunny rabbit shadow can you make on the wall opposite her right ear? (Huge.)

Mark Ashworth lent his much-needed technical and musical assistance, including manipulating data on his computer in ways that would make Mr. Wizard jealous. In addition, Mark helped to create most of the music illustrations used in this book.

My brother, Dick Probasco, also helped with illustrations, and his son, Brent, rendered the "foot" that more or less serves as the linchpin of Chapter 3.

While I've been busy explaining to parents how to teach their kids about music, my wife, Jan, the real parent-music teacher of our family, made sure that son Brad practiced his trombone and sold his quota of band pizzas and subs; reminded daughter Erika to take her flute to her flute lesson—something any savvy parent-music teacher will tell you cannot be taken for granted; and didn't laugh out loud when son Dana, the trumpet and French horn player, declared recently he had discovered an exciting new musical group—the Beatles.

Most important, Jan has seen to it that our children have received the nurturing and love they needed in order to grow up not to be detriments to society. For that I am most grateful.

CONTENTS

INTRODUCTION

Hold it!

I know it's considered "uncool" to read Introductions, but before you rush off to Chapter 1, please take a few minutes to glance at the paragraphs that follow. In them I have laid out what this book is all about, which could save you valuable time in case you have picked up the wrong book.

For example, if you woke up this morning and found a funny-looking, big-eared, flying rat in your bedroom closet and you're looking for ways to remove this "radar-guided" mammal from your house, you could probably benefit from knowing that this book contains very little guidance on that subject. Virtually none, in fact.

On the other hand, if your home is basically "bat-less," and you are interested in helping your child learn about music, read on.

This book is designed to help you teach your child about music—even if you have little or no musical training yourself. You will find information to aid you in teaching your child the basics of reading music; getting your child started making music by playing an instrument or singing in a choir or other musical group; and developing a listening program to broaden your child's musical horizons.

If your child wants to become the next Wynton Marsalis, Beverly Sills, or Paul Simon, there is a chapter that discusses careers in music. On the other hand, if your child wants to become a professional late-night TV song stylist, you can skip the book. Just buy him an electric kazoo and change his name to something that sounds like an organic cleaning compound. As far as I know, that's about all there is to a career in the mail-order recording industry.

There is information on teaching materials, including music-related supplies, games, computer software, and even a new video game accessory that claims to teach your child how to play the piano! By the way, this is the only video game I know of that does not have an exploding turnip as a central figure, although it does feature an option that allows your child to splatter ducks with tomatoes by playing correct notes!

This book is "non-graded"—that is, no reference is made to specific grade or age levels. In general, the book covers the kind of musical knowledge and skills children should receive from about the age of seven or eight through junior high school or middle school.

I have used the pronoun "he" throughout the book, in reference to the child. It is just too confusing to switch back and forth from "he" to "she." Hope I haven't offended anyone.

Well, that's about it for the Introduction. It all pretty much boils down to this: if you are looking for information on pest control, you need to visit another Dewey Decimal classification. I would suggest something in the 600's . . . around 638, maybe. No, that's Beekeeping. Well, you'll just have to look around.

If, on the other hand, you want to learn how to become a parent-music teacher, go to Chapter 1. I'll join you in a minute. I have to check something first. I think I heard a "bleep" coming from the bedroom closet.

1.

FIRST THINGS FIRST

"I don't know much about music, but I know what I like."

There is nothing wrong with "knowing what you like" without knowing *why*, exactly. Music is, after all, an acquired form of personal expression. (I know this because it says so a little later in the chapter!)

Think how much better it would be, however, if your child made choices about music in his life from an informed perspective —not just based on what his friends like or what the MTV vee-jay says he's *supposed* to like. This book aims to give you the tools you need to help your child learn more about music.

Before the actual teaching begins, we need to answer a few questions. What is music? Why should your child study it? What role should *you* play in your child's music education? These are all good questions. Here are some answers.

THE UNIVERSAL LANGUAGE

Music is sometimes called "The Universal Language," which is strange since it's neither universal nor a language.

Think about it. To be universal, music would have to be the same all over the world. This is obviously not so. In fact, not only does music vary from country to country, but even within cultures, musical tastes vary widely.

As for being a language, if you think this is so, try walking into a filling station and asking for the key to the bathroom using only a bagpipe. My guess is, you will get strange looks, blank stares, or laughter. What you won't get is the key to the bathroom.

The truth is, firing up the Vienna Philharmonic every time you want someone to pass the salt at the dinner table is neither practical nor efficient. It's probably not even in good taste. So if music isn't the universal language, what is it?

BOTH ART AND SCIENCE

Music is "the art and science of combining sounds to form an emotionally expressive composition." For a dictionary-style definition, that's not bad. "But," you may ask, "just what in the heck does it mean?"

It means that music appeals to both the creative and to the logical aspects of human nature—making it a unique (and I believe necessary) part of your child's education. In other words, the study of music involves using both verbal (left brain) and non-verbal (right brain) processes. This is important, because studies have shown that exercising both halves of the brain simultaneously results in a child with a symmetrical head. At least I *think* that's what those studies have shown.

Scientific theories aside, one would think music would have to be more than just a way to get your brain to do pushups. It is.

AN ACQUIRED FORM OF PERSONAL EXPRESSION

Music is an acquired form of personal expression. Not only does preference in musical style vary from culture to culture and from generation to generation, it also varies from person to person.

As a parent, you should not expect your child to like the music you like. Your role as a parent-music teacher is *not* to teach your child which music is "good" and which is "bad," but to help your chid become "musically literate" so that he can decide for himself.

Ultimately, you will find that the more your child knows about music, including how to read, how to sing or play an instrument, and how to listen to music with understanding, the better prepared he will be to make important choices later in life as an "informed consumer of music."

MUSIC HAS INTRINSIC VALUE

The intrinsic value of music refers to the fact that music has worth of its own—a worth not dependent on external factors. To put it simply, music contributes uniquely to the human experience and is vital to your child's comprehensive, balanced education. Learning about music enhances your child's life in ways no other type of learning can accomplish.

By the way, the fact that music has intrinsic value doesn't mean you can order a cheeseburger at your favorite fast food restaurant and pay for it with a couple quick choruses of "Louie, Louie." That won't work—unless, of course, you put on a really good show!

MUSIC CONTRIBUTES TO OTHER AREAS

Learning to read music facilitates other basic reading skills such as oral reading, reading comprehension, and reading vocabulary.

The study of music teaches concentration, memory skills, alertness, and self-discipline. Since music is based on the physics of sound and employs the fundamentals of math in its written notation, it also contributes to achievement in those areas.

Music fosters creativity and imagination, aesthetic taste, a positive self-image, and the development of psychomotor and social skills.

In short, music contributes to the making of the whole child.

MUSIC IS PART OF YOUR CHILD'S LIFE

Whatever it is or isn't, music *is* part of your child's everyday life. Children begin to form their preferences for music early on.

The sooner you take an active role in your child's music education, the better.

On the other hand, if what you hear coming from your child's stereo sounds like a cat strapped to the blade of a mulching mower, take heart. It's never too late to have a positive impact on your child's taste in music. You may not be able to teach an old dog new tricks, but you *can* teach an old dog new music.

I know, I said you shouldn't expect your child to like the music you like and that he will develop his own preferences based on personal taste. That's true. Still, if the only music your child ever listens to sounds like a demolition derby in a blender, there is probably room for some variety in his record collection. Wouldn't you agree?

THE SCHOOL MUSIC PROGRAM

Nearly all children study music as part of the school curriculum. In the early grades, music is sometimes taught by a classroom teacher, but most schools today employ music specialists for the job.

Elementary School Music Programs

Music in the elementary school is designed around a program of general music. The elementary general music teacher will probably be the first music specialist with whom your child comes in contact. The general music class meets once or twice a week and consists mostly of singing, movement (dancing), playing a variety of rhythm and melody-producing instruments, and listening.

Some elementary schools have a choir; the general music teacher often directs this group. In about the fifth or sixth grade (sometimes earlier), other music specialists come into the picture: the band teacher and the strings (orchestra) teacher. Not all children join band or orchestra, so your child will see these specialists only if he elects to join one of these groups.

Two Teaching Methods

Many elementary school general music curricula utilize at least some elements of two innovative teaching methods imported from

Europe. The following brief descriptions of these methods may prove helpful to you if your child's music teacher uses them in the classroom. If nothing else, the teacher will be impressed when you drop these names into casual conversation during open house!

As a parent-music teacher, it is not necessary for you to understand either of these teaching systems completely. If you want to know more, there are books on both methods available at most public libraries, or you can ask your child's music teacher to direct you to sources of additional information. You can also write to the supporting organizations listed in Appendix B.

The Kodaly Method

A Hungarian composer and teacher, Zoltan Kodaly (1882-1967), believed that all children should be taught to hear music with understanding and be able to read music fluently. The method that bears his name is designed to teach young children through singing and a series of hand signs and rhythm symbols, and to aid children in developing an understanding of tonal and rhythmic relationships. (You may recall the use of Kodaly's hand signs in the movie *Close Encounters of the Third Kind*.)

The Kodaly system also uses what is known as the "movable do" system. In the "movable do" system, the syllables "do, re, mi, fa, sol, la, ti, do" are used for teaching pitch relationships and "do" is always the home tone. In other words, the pitch for "do" changes, depending on which pitches are contained in the song being sung.

The most important thing to remember about the Kodaly system is that all musical learning is derived from songs. The music comes first, the understanding later. Children are taught first by *rote*, then by *note*.

The Orff Approach

Carl Orff (1895-1982), a contemporary German composer and teacher, developed the *Schulwerk* (Music for Children) system. The Orff Schulwerk system is based on the unity of speech, movement, and music, which Orff called "elemental music." In the Orff system, all children actively participate in the making and creating of music.

Orff believed rhythm is the most natural response to music and the common denominator of the three components of speech, movement, and music. The Orff approach emphasizes the use of special "Orff instruments," which are used to accompany singing. The Orff system also involved a great deal of improvisation and musical creativity by students.

MIDDLE AND JUNIOR HIGH SCHOOL MUSIC PROGRAMS

By middle school or junior high, specialization in music begins. If your child is in band, orchestra, or choir, he probably won't be in the general music class.

Sometimes even within groups there is further specialization; i.e., one or more choruses, bands, or orchestras, organized according to grade level or experience and ability.

Some middle schools and junior high schools also offer classes in piano (keyboard) and guitar. Others include piano and guitar instruction as part of the general music class; still others don't offer it at all. Check with your school for particulars about the programs.

HIGH SCHOOL MUSIC PROGRAMS

The high school music program is the most specialized of all. Most high schools have a choir, a marching band, and a concert band. Many also sponsor an orchestra, a jazz ensemble, a show choir, and a basketball pep band. Some offer a class in music theory or music appreciation, and a few have piano or guitar labs.

Many high schools offer no "general music" (music appreciation) class. This is unfortunate because if we truly believe that music education is for all children, we should not leave out those who choose not to participate in music performance groups at the high school level.

YOUR ROLE AS A PARENT-MUSIC TEACHER

In order for music to be part of your child's education, he must study it. In school, the general music teacher is the one who will introduce the study of music into your child's life.

But that's not enough. You need to be able to encourage and guide your child's music education, just as you help with his math education, social studies education, and so forth.

It's your job to help your child become an informed music consumer. This task includes, among other things, helping him learn to read music. Music reading is usually introduced as part of the general music class, beginning in the second or third grade. Your role is to reinforce what is taught at school and to help your child practice at home so his reading skills will flourish. If your child is older and has not been introduced to music reading, don't worry. It's never too late to start.

You should also encourage your child to sing and to learn to play an instrument. There are so many instruments avilable these days, I am hard pressed to think of a child who couldn't find *something* he wants to play, whether piano, guitar, a band instrument, or an orchestra instrument.

You should reinforce your child's listening skills by making sure he hears a variety of musical styles. Even though this is done as part of the general music class in school, you need to incorporate musical variety into your child's home listening habits, or his musical focus will tend to be very narrow.

All this is part of your role as PARENT-MUSIC TEACHER. As a parent-music teacher, your influence on your child's attitude about music education is just as important as your influence on his attitude about education in general.

HOW TO BE A PARENT-MUSIC TEACHER

Being a parent-*teacher* probably isn't a new role for you. If you are a parent, you are a teacher. It goes with the territory. If your background in music is weak, however, becoming a parent-music teacher may seem a little scary. Don't worry. Music teachers are not "anointed," they're trained. You can learn about music and pass your knowledge on to your child.

I will be talking to *you* in this book—not your child. It is your job to talk to your child. You may want to explain things a little differently than I do when you teach your child. That's OK. It's best, however, to present material in the same sequence as it is presented in each chapter.

Read through the book before you begin working with your child. Study the three chapters (2-4) on music reading especially closely to make sure you understand everything presented there. Complete the exercises yourself before asking your child to do them.

Since you will be working with a music professional (the school music teacher), don't hesitate to contact your teaching "buddy" when you have questions about the material in this book. Some of the rhythmic elements, for example, are easier to show than they are to tell. You and your child might benefit from a brief musical "demonstration." Most music teachers would be delighted to know of your interest in your child's music education and will be happy to oblige.

HOW THIS BOOK IS ORGANIZED AND HOW TO USE IT

The book covers three main areas of music education: Music Reading (Chapters 2, 3, and 4); Music Making (Chapter 5); and Listening to Music (Chapter 6). Chapter 7 discusses careers in music and Chapter 8 contains information on helpful teaching materials related to music.

I urge you to work with your child in all three areas at the same time. In other words, your child should learn to read, make, and listen to music all at once. Start at the beginning of each section and work toward the end. Since Chapter 2 deals with reading "notes" and Chapter 3 with reading "rhythm," start teaching those chapters simultaneously, but wait to begin Chapter 4 until completing both Chapters 2 and 3.

When the book calls for you to show your child a musical example, you can use the book or you can draw your own examples, using the figures in the book to guide you. Refer to Chapter 8 for information on teaching supplies you can buy—items like music marker boards and staff paper—before starting the sections on music reading.

There is no hurry to finish this book in a set period of time.

Depending on your child's age and background, it may take several months or years. For example, the information on music reading covers material that is taught in school from about Grade 2 through Grade 6 or 7. An older child will go through this material faster than a younger one, but that doesn't mean he will have learned to read music. Learning to read music, like learning to read language, requires drill and repetition as well as enthusiasm.

The exercises you will find in this book are specific activities you can do with your child. Try to create variations on the exercises so the necessary drill and repetition can occur painlessly.

Whatever you do, don't make your child's home music lessons too long. School music classes usually last only about thirty minutes. Teaching (and drilling) one or two music-reading exercises and listening to and discussing one recorded piece of music can easily take twenty to thirty minutes. Add that to the time your child might spend making music—either through singing at home or taking piano, guitar, or other instrument lessons—and you have a pretty full music curriculum for your child.

Finally, it isn't necessary to teach music every day. You might designate one evening a week as "music night" and work on music then, or you might spread it out over two or three nights, with music reading one night, listening another, and music-making on a third. That's up to you. After all *you're* the PARENT-MUSIC TEACHER!

2.

MUSIC READING: NOTES

This chapter begins the section of the book that deals with teaching your child how to read music. You should begin this chapter and Chapter 3 simultaneously, flipping back and forth. If your child goes through one chapter faster than the other, that's fine. There's only one place where information from Chapter 3 is required to understand something in Chapter 2, and that place is clearly marked.

NOTE, TONE, OR PITCH?

Music terminology can be confusing. Many "music words" seem to be interchangeable. The words *tone, note,* and *pitch,* for example, can all be used to describe a musical *sound.* To add to the confusion, many "music words" have different meanings, depending on context.

In this book the word *note* can refer to a musical "sound" or to a written "symbol." A note's *name* is its *pitch* (or sound); its *type* refers to *duration* (how long the note lasts). As you will learn later in this chapter and in Chapter 3, the location of a note on the staff tells us its *name* or *pitch* and the shape of a note tells us its *type* or *duration.*

Now if we are to spend the next three chapters learning one

set of skills, one obvious question needs to be answered first: why bother?

WHY LEARN TO READ MUSIC?

In some cultures, notably Indian, music is mostly "improvised" —made up as you go along—and music reading is not needed and not taught. Improvisation also occurs in certain types of Western music, such as jazz, but for the most part Western musical traditions rely on written notation.

If your child is to learn about music in Western society, he must learn to read music notation. Music-reading skills should be part of your child's education just as regular reading skills are. After all, language is part of your child's daily life, and he needs to learn how to read, write, and make words. Music is also part of your child's daily life so he needs to learn how to read, write, and make music.

THE MUSICAL ALPHABET

Before your child can learn to read words, he must become familiar with the alphabet. It's the same with reading music. Before your child can learn to read written music notation, he must gain some facility with the musical alphabet.

The musical alphabet consists of the first seven letters of the regular alphabet:

A—B—C—D—E—F—G

After G, we start again at A:

A—B—C—D—E—F—G—A—B—C—D—E—F—G, etc.

The next few exercises will help your child gain some facility with the musical alphabet and will make music-note reading much easier.

Exercise 2:1—Have your child say the first seven letters of the alphabet in order: A—B—C—D—E—F—G. Then have him say them backward: G—F—E—D—C—B—A.

Some children find this difficult because it's not something they normally do. However, since musical notes can be written in any order, it's important for your child to learn to say the musical alphabet forward and backward.

Have your child practice saying the line below. (Don't let him read it. He must do it from memory.)

A—B—C—D—E—F—G—(pause)—G—F—E—D—C—B—A

Try it yourself. In fact, it might be fun for the two of you to have a contest to see who can do it fastest and with the fewest mistakes.

"Forward & Backward" vs. "Up & Down"

You will notice in the exercises that follow, I have substituted the word "up" for "forward" and the word "down" for "backward." The reason, as you will see later, is that note names are based on vertical placement on the musical staff (up or down). I don't want your child to confuse terms when actual note name reading starts.

Your child will probably know what you mean when you use the terms, but if he seems confused, explain that "up" means "forward" and "down" means "backward." He'll catch on quickly.

Exercise 2:2—Remember that the musical alphabet goes back to A after G. Have your child say this:

A—B—C—D—E—F—G—A—B—C—D—E—F—G—A—B—
C—etc.

Have your child do as many repetitions of A—B—C—D—E—F—G as he can do in one breath.

Then have him do it down (backward), again with as many repetitions as possible in one breath.

Exercise 2:3—In this exercise, ask your child to say the musical alphabet up (forward) and down (backward), each time starting on a different letter. For example:

C—D—E—F—G—A—B—C—(pause)—C—B—A—G—F—E
—D—C

or

F—G—A—B—C—D—E—F—(pause)—F—E—D—C—B—A
—G—F

Do this, starting on each of the seven letters, making sure your child always says *A* after reaching *G* on the way up, and *G* after *A* on the way down.

Exercise 2:4—Now have your child say the musical alphabet up and down, starting on any letter, and skipping every other one. For example:

A—C—E—G—B—D—F—A—(pause)—A—F—D—B—G—E
—C—A

or

B—D—F—A—C—E—G—B—(pause)—B—G—E—C—A—F
—D—B

Notice that we still say at least eight letters up and eight letters down. Naturally, your child can say more than eight up and down, by following the rule for repeating—that is, start again at *A* after reaching *G*.

Don't try to do all this at once. It can become confusing to your child and it may take several sessions before your child has really mastered "saying" the musical alphabet.

With enough practice, however, your child will soon be able to say the musical alphabet up and down as fast as he can count numbers up and down.

As soon as your child has mastered verbalizing the musical alphabet, it's time to go on to the next step: Learning the basic symbols of music notation.

GOOD BOYS, HUNGRY COWS, AND OTHER MUSICAL NONSENSE

Before we go any further, I need to bring up the use of memory aids to learn note names. If you learned to read music as a child, you might have been taught phrases like: "Every Good Boy Does Fine" or "All Cows Eat Grass" to help you remember the names of the lines and spaces on the staff. Many music teachers still use this system, and it is possible that your child has already been introduced to music reading through the use of such memory aids.

The problem with these devices is that they add an unnecessary step to the learning process. It's kind of like learning the alphabet by the numbers (1 = A, 2 = B, and so on).

I don't recommend using these phrases. Instead, concentrate on teaching your child the alphabetical relationship between adjacent lines and spaces, which you will learn about in the next few paragraphs. In the long run, your child will learn to read music better and faster.

DRAWING MUSICAL SYMBOLS

You will notice that many of the exercises call for your child to write (or draw) music. Children would rather *do something* than listen to someone talk, and drawing music symbols helps to reinforce learning.

For Exercise 2:5, your child should use a blank sheet of paper. For all the other exercises, you can use blank paper and draw your own staff, or you can buy an inexpensive tablet of music staff paper (from a music store or catalog). For about $15, you can get a large laminated chart-size staff that can be used over and over with a dry-wipe marker. (If you have access to a laminator, you can laminate your own staff paper and use it with a dry wipe marker, available at most office supply or educational supply stores.) See Chapter 8 for more information on teaching resources such as staff paper, etc.

THE STAFF

Music is written on a *staff*, consisting of five parallel lines and the four spaces between them (Figure 1).

Figure 1

Exercise 2:5—On a blank sheet of paper, have your child draw a staff like the one in Figure 1. It doesn't matter how far apart the lines are—they just need to be parallel. If your child has trouble drawing straight lines, let him use a ruler. (Remember: This is music class, not art class!)

Notice that a staff looks sort of like a ladder. Depending on your child's age, you may want to refer to it as a "music ladder." Later, you can substitute the word "staff" for "ladder."

CLEF SIGNS

Once we have our staff, we need to add a *clef sign*. There are two clef signs, the G or Treble Clef and the F or Bass (pronounced "base") Clef. The clef we use determines the letter names of the lines and spaces on the staff. When a *note* is placed on a line or space, it takes on the name of that line or space.

G Clef

The G or Treble Clef is used for the higher pitches (the right-hand part on the piano). Notice how the G Clef begins by curling around the second line of the staff (Figure 2). That's the G line. A note placed on the second line is called G. If you use your imagination, I suppose you could say the G Clef looks sort of like a fancy letter G. I think it looks more like a girl I dated in junior high, but that's only my opinion.

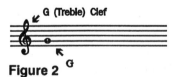

Figure 2

Exercise 2:6—Have your child draw several G Clefs on staff paper. Be sure he starts just below the second line and curves around as shown in Figure 2. Point to the second line and ask, "What's the name of this line?" (*G.*)

Once we know where *G* is, figuring out the names of the other lines and spaces is easy. That's because the lines and spaces are named "alphabetically" from bottom to top (Figure 3).

D E F G A B C D E F G

Figure 3

Notice that the note placed on the space above second-line *G* is *A*. (Remember, we go back to *A* after we reach *G*). The note on the line above *A* is *B*. The note on the space above *B* is *C*; and so on all the way up to the note on the space above the top line, *G*.

Going down from second-line *G*, we simply say the musical alphabet backward. The space below second-line *G* is *F*; the bottom line is *E*; and the space below the staff, *D*.

Exercise 2:7—Ask your child to draw a G Clef on a staff. Take a pencil and point to a line or space and have your child tell you its name. If he's not sure, have him "spell" up or down from second-line *G*.

Do this exercise until your child can say aloud the names of the lines and spaces from memory, without using the *G* line as a reference point.

If your child has learned to say the music alphabet forward and backward, he will find it easy to name lines and spaces in either direction by "spelling" forward or backward. If he has trouble, review the music alphabet.

F Clef

The F or Bass Clef indicates the lower pitches (left-hand part on the piano). Notice how the F Clef starts on the fourth line from the bottom, curves up to the top line, then back down (Figure 4). Look at the two dots on either side of the fourth line. Can you guess the letter name of the fourth line? Did you guess "F"? Good. You're right!

F (Bass) Clef

Figure 4

Exercise 2:8—Have your child draw several F Clefs on staff paper. Make sure he starts on the fourth line, curves up to the top line, then back down again. Also, make sure he remembers the two dots.

Even though the lines and spaces have different names with the F Clef, they are still named alphabetically from bottom to top. With the F Clef, the space above fourth line *F* is *G*; the line above that, *A*, and so on (Figure 5).

F G A B C D E F G A B

Figure 5

Exercise 2:9—Have your child draw an F Clef on staff paper. Take a pencil and point to a line or space and ask him to name it. Do this with all the lines and spaces in random order.

If your child can't remember the name of a line or space, have him spell up or down from fourth line *F*. Now I hope you can see why it is important for your child to be able to say the musical alphabet forward and backward!

Exercise 2:10—This exercise is a variation on 7 and 9. Ask your child to draw a G Clef on one staff and an F Clef on the other. Call out the name of a note, *A, B, C, D, E, F,* or *G,* and then either G Clef or F Clef.

Your child should then "draw" that note on the appropriate staff. His notes should look like the ones shown in Figures 3 and 5 —like slightly flattened donuts—making sure the line goes through the middle of any note that is supposed to be on a line, and that any note on a space is centered between two lines.

Also, remember that *D, E, F,* and *G* in the G Clef and *F, G, A,* and B in the F Clef appear more than once. If you call out any of these notes, there are two possible right answers.

GRAND STAFF

Music for most instruments and for singers is written on one staff—with either a G Clef or an F Clef. Piano music, however, is written on two staffs bracketed together. When a G Clef staff and an F Clef staff are bracketed together, as shown in Figure 6, that's called a *grand staff*.

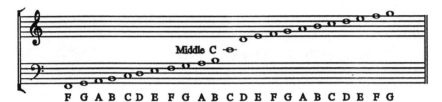

Figure 6

Notice the new note, *middle C*. It's called middle C because it's in the . . . well, I guess it's obvious, isn't it?

Exercise 2:11—Have your child draw a Grand Staff, draw in all the notes, and label them as shown in Figure 6.

Figure 7 shows the location on a piano keyboard of all the notes you have learned so far. Notice that the notes repeat themselves on the piano keyboard just as they do in the musical alphabet. A full piano keyboard has eighty-eight keys. The section shown in Figure 7 is only a small part of the middle section of a full piano keyboard.

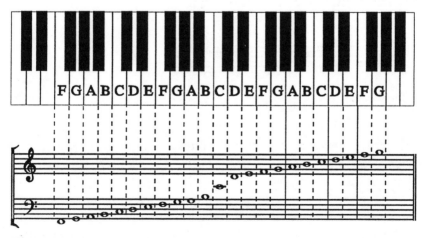

Figure 7

Exercise 2:12—If you have a piano or an electric keyboard, ask your child to locate and play all the notes shown in Figure 7. By the way, it doesn't matter whether or not your piano or electric keyboard has eighty-eight keys. Just locate the *C* closest to the middle and call that "middle *C*." If you need help locating *C*, look at Figure 7 again. Notice that *C* is the white key just to the left of the two black keys. Notice also that only white keys are played for this exercise. The black keys will make a joyful noise later.

The notes in the F Clef sound lower in pitch than the notes in the G Clef. On the piano, the right hand usually plays the G Clef notes and the left hand plays the F Clef notes. Middle C can be played by either hand.

LEGER LINES

There are many more notes than can be shown on the five lines and four spaces of the staff. To show these other notes, short lines called *leger lines* are drawn above or below the staff. The same alphabetical order is used to name leger lines (and the spaces between them) as is used with the regular staff.

Figure 8 shows some leger lines and notes in both G Clef and F Clef.

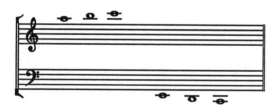

Figure 8

The number of leger lines could go on forever (but rarely does). Four or five leger lines in either direction are usually more than enough.

Exercise 2:13 — Have your child practice drawing some leger lines above and below the staff. Have him add notes to the leger lines and label them in both G Clef and F Clef. (See Figure 8 for help.)

A common mistake children make is to draw three or four leger lines, then put a note on the first or second. Rule: Never draw more leger lines than you need. The note should always be on the last leger line or just above it (or below it, if you're drawing leger lines below the staff).

OVERLAPPING NOTES

With leger lines, some notes overlap between the two staffs (G Clef and F Clef). For example, middle *C* is on the first leger line below the G Clef and on the first leger line above the F Clef. Figure 9 shows middle *C* and some other notes that overlap.

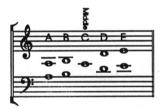

Figure 9

Exercise 2:14—Go over the notes in Figure 9 with your child and make sure he understands about notes that overlap. If you have a piano or keyboard, have him play the notes, so he can see (and hear) that the overlapping notes are the same. For example: *A* on the top line of the F Clef is the same as *A* on the second leger line down from the G Clef.

By the way, with a Grand Staff (piano music), there is normally no need for leger lines above the F Clef or below the G Clef. This is because notes above middle C automatically go on the G Clef and notes below middle C automatically go on the F Clef.

By now you and your child should be able to identify the names of the notes in both the G and F Clefs, as well as up to four leger lines above and below both clefs.

SHARPS, FLATS, AND NATURALS

Up to this point all music has been written with *natural* notes —*A, B, C, D, E, F,* and *G.* There are also some other notes besides the natural notes that can be sung and played: *sharps* and *flats.*

Sharp and flat notes are represented by the black keys on the piano. Since they are easier to understand there, that's where we will start (Figure 10).

Figure 10

You will notice that there are no black keys (and therefore no sharps or flats) between *B* and *C* or between *E* and *F.*

In written music, sharp notes are marked by a sharp sign (#). The sharp note above (to the right of) A on the keyboard is called "A sharp" (A#). *A#* is located between *A* and *B* on the piano keyboard and sounds higher than *A,* but lower than *B* (Figure 11).

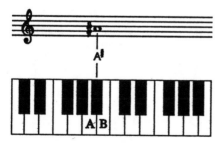

Figure 11

Flat notes are marked with a flat sign (♭). The flat note below (to the left of) *B* is called "B flat" (*B*♭). *B*♭ sounds lower than *B* (but higher than *A*) and is located between *A* and *B* on the piano keyboard (Figure 12).

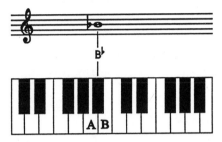

Figure 12

Hold it a second! Didn't I just say that the note between *A* and *B* was *A#*? Now, I'm saying the note between *A* and *B* is *B♭*! What's the matter—can't I make up my mind? How can this be?

Here's how it works. All black keys on the piano keyboard have two names. The key between *A* and *B* is both *A#* AND *B♭*. The key sounds the same when you play it, but it has two different names in written notation (Figure 13).

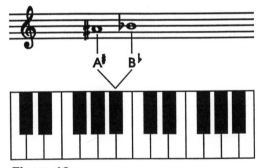

Figure 13

Notes that sound the same but have different names are said to be *enharmonic*. Therefore, *A#* and *B♭* are *enharmonic*.

Exercise 2:15—Go over Figures 10-13 with your child. Make sure he understands that a sharp is higher than a natural note of the same name (*A#* is higher than *A*); and that a flat is lower than a natural note of the same name (*B♭* is lower than *B*).

Also make sure your child understands that all sharps also

have a flat name (and vice versa), and that when two notes sound alike but have different names they are said to be enharmonic.

We have seen that on the staff, sharps and flats are indicated with either a sharp sign (#) or a flat sign (♭) in front of the note that is to be "sharped" or "flatted." When you say the name of the note, however, you say the letter name first and the word "sharp" or "flat" second. For example, in Figure 14, the first note is called "F sharp," not "sharp F"; and the second is "B flat," not "flat B."

Figure 14

Exercise 2:16—Have your child draw the notes *A#*, *B♭*, *C#*, *D♭*, *F#*, and *G♭* on staff paper. Have him do it in both clefs. Make sure he puts the sharp or flat sign before the note. Have him say aloud the name of each note he has drawn and make sure he says the letter name first, followed by "sharp" or "flat."

You may remember that a note without a sharp or flat in front of it is called a *natural* note. Sometimes, we put a *natural sign* in front of a note that was previously "sharped" or "flatted," in order to cancel the sharp or flat. Figure 15 shows how the "natural" sign is used to cancel a "sharp" or "flat."

Figure 15

Exercise 2:17—Go over Figure 15 with your child, making sure he understands that a natural sign cancels a sharp or flat. In other words, "*A natural*" and "*A*" are the same note.

Since the black keys on the piano each have two names (a sharp name and a flat name), your child might wonder which one we should use in written music. The answer is: "It depends on the 'key' of the music." More on that in just a moment, but first . . .

SPECIAL PLACES—B & C AND E & F

Do you remember that there are no black keys between the notes *B* and *C* or between *E* and *F*? (See Figure 10.) That doesn't mean you can't have a *B#* or a *C♭*, or an *E#* or *F♭*. The truth is, *B#* is really *C* and *C♭* is really *B*. And *E#* is really *F*, and *F♭* is really *E*.

Confused? No need to be. Just remember that since there are no black keys in these two places, the next key up or down (in this case, a white key) becomes the sharp or flat (Figure 16).

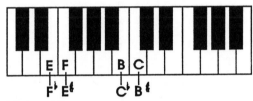

Figure 16

The only thing that is different is that these notes don't have two names as the black keys do. (Actually, they do, but that gets into a part of music theory not covered in this book.)

ACCIDENTALS

When a note is changed by adding a sharp, flat, or natural, it is called an *accidental*. A change made by an accidental lasts until the end of the measure in which it occurs.

Time out! Here's that place I told you about where a "rhythm" concept must be mastered before a "note" concept can be taught. If your child has not yet learned the term *measure*, turn to Chapter 3 and look it up in the section called Bar Lines and Measures.

And now, back to our regularly scheduled lesson . . .

In other words, if you have a *B* and you add a flat to it, making it *B* , then all *B*'s in the entire measure would become *B* . At the beginning of the next measure, the note goes back to its original name and status.

KEYS AND KEY SIGNATURES

Up to this point, sharps, flats, and naturals have been written into the music as needed. There is an easier way to indicate which notes are to be sharp or flat. It's called a *key signature*. A key signature comes immediately after the clef sign and tells which notes are to be sharp or flat. (When there are no sharps or flats, that key signature is called "C.")

A key signature can have anywhere from 0 to 7 sharps or flats in it. It *never* has a mixture of sharps and flats, and the sharps or flats always occur in the same order—*B, E, A, D, G, C, F* for flats, and *F, C, G, D, A, E, B* for sharps.

Figure 17 shows an example of a key signature. This particular key signature has three flats in it. They are *B♭, E♭,* and *A♭*. This means that in this song *all B's, all E's,* and all *A's* are "flatted." In other words, when you see a *B,* you play *B♭*; when you see an *E,* you play *E♭*; and when you see an *A,* you play *A♭*. Unlike accidentals, notes sharped or flatted by key signatures stay that way through the entire piece. Unless, of course, they are altered by an accidental, in which case . . . OK, I'll shut up. I know it's starting to get confusing. Take a look at Figure 17.

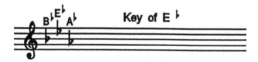

Figure 17

Notice that each of the three flats in the key signature are on the line or space that names the note they flat. Of course, even though the *B♭* is on the middle line, all *B's,* including those on leger lines, are to be "flatted." This is true for all flats and sharps in all key signatures.

Figure 18 shows all the flat and sharp key signatures. Remember: This is the only way they appear. If there is *one* flat it is *always*

B♭. If there are *two* sharps, they are *always F#* and *C#*. No excep-tions—ever. Sharps and flats always follow the same order. (Isn't it nice to know there is some order to music?)

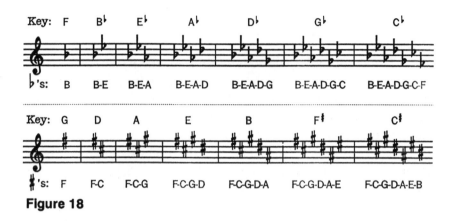

Figure 18

Exercise 2:18—Go over all the sharp and flat key signatures with your child. Help him memorize the name of the key as well as the names of the sharps or flats in each key signature.

If he doesn't notice it himself, point out that the "order" of sharps F-C-G-D-A-E-B, is the reverse of the order of flats, B-E-A-D-G-C-F. I could tell you why that is, but we would never get out of this chapter. Let's just call it one of music's little "miracles."

MAJOR SCALES

Take another look at Figure 18. Notice the group of eight notes following each key signature. Notice how the first note in each case is the same as the name of the key. This note is called the *tonic*. If you start on the first (or *tonic*) note of a key and go up through the musical alphabet (making sure you play all flat or sharp notes indicated by the key signature), and stop when you ar-rive back at the beginning note name, you have a *major scale*. (Yes, there is something called a *minor scale* too, but we don't want to get into it in this book.)

Remember, if there are sharps or flats in the key signature, the affected notes must be played sharp or flat in order for the scale to sound right.

Exercise 2:19—Have your child name and play the notes in the major scale for each of the key signatures shown in Figure 18. This will take some time to learn. Make sure he knows which notes are to be flat or sharp—and be especially careful when it comes to tricky ones like *E#* (really *F*); *B#* (really *C*); *C♭* (really *B*); and *F♭* (really *E*).

Though the notes will sound different, the pattern will sound the same. If he does it enough times, your child should quickly learn the "sound" of a major scale. Just make sure your child checks the key signature carefully and plays the appropriate notes flat or sharp as called for. Refer to Figures 13 and 18 if necessary.

Congratulations! This completes the note-reading portion of this book. As soon as your child finishes Chapter 3, you can put the icing on the "music-reading" cake by reading Chapter 4.

3.

MUSIC READING: RHYTHM

Almost every child responds to *rhythm* in music. Rhythm causes us to snap our fingers, tap our feet, or "get up and boogie." Learning to read and understand rhythm in written music is not hard . . . as long as you jump in feet first.

COUNTING BEATS—FOOT TAPPING

The basic component of *rhythm* is the *beat*. Learning to keep a steady *beat* requires a "system" for counting. The one I like best is called the "down-up" foot tap.

Learning the "down-up" foot tap, like learning to say the musical alphabet, must be mastered before your child can learn to read rhythms.

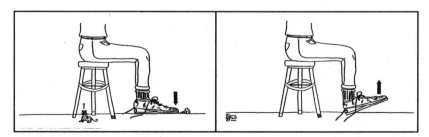

Figure 19

Exercise 3:1—Ask your child to begin tapping his foot in a steady "down-up" pattern (Figure 19). Either foot is OK. Your child will probably like to keep his heel on the floor and tap his toe down and up. Most children prefer this method. Some children are more comfortable tapping the heel. Either way is fine.

Have your child say "down" as his foot goes down and "up" when it comes back up. The motion should be almost jerky. It shouldn't be smooth or round. Have your child tap his foot "down-up" until he keeps a steady pattern (or until he gets tired — whichever comes first).

Exercise 3:2—As soon as your child can keep a steady beat without slowing down or speeding up, have him try to tap his foot in time to recorded music. Try to pick music that has a beat that's easy to hear and that is steady (doesn't slow down or speed up). Music that is too fast will be hard to tap "down-up" to, so it's best to find something that's moderately slow.

Some children seem to pick up the "down-up" foot tap very quickly. For others it takes longer. Don't be discouraged if your child has a few coordination problems at first.

When I'm teaching the "down-up" foot tap and a child says he "just can't do it," I always ask if he can walk and chew gum at the same time. The answer, for most children, is an emphatic "yes." Then I tell them that if they can walk and chew gum at the same time, they can do the "down-up" foot tap.

For some reason, children are usually satisfied with this answer. There's absolutely no logic to it whatsoever—walking and chewing gum have nothing to do with tapping your foot—but rarely do I get an objection when I say this. (Not counting, of course, the kid who immediately stands up with a wad of bubble gum in his mouth, takes two steps, and smacks into a wall just to make me look bad!)

Once your child can keep a steady "down-up" foot tap, have him try to reverse it and start with "up." The rhythm now will be "up-down, up-down, etc." Actually, for most children, starting on "up" is easier. At any rate, have your child practice both the "down-up" foot tap and the "up-down" foot tap. (This is one of those musical things that doesn't make much sense now, but when we get to learn about syncopation you will be glad your child learned to do it.)

"LIAR, LIAR, PANTS ON FIRE!"

In the next few pages I'm going to tell you how many beats each type of note or rest gets. What I tell you will not exactly be a lie, but it won't be the truth either. You see, the actual number of beats a note or rest gets depends on something else—something we haven't discussed yet. I don't want to tell you what that "something" is, because it would spoil the surprise. So, for now, let's assume everything I tell you is the truth. The "truth" is I'm lying. Go figure.

DURATION—NOTES AND RESTS

The two basic symbols of music notation are the *note* and the *rest*. A *note* indicates a musical sound; a *rest* indicates silence.

Just as the position of a note on the staff indicates its pitch, the shape of a note or rest (no matter where it is located on the staff) tells us how long the musical sound or silence should last. The length of time a note or rest lasts is measured in *beats* and is called its *duration*.

A *beat* consists of one "down-up" or "up-down" foot tap. The reason a beat is either "down-up" or "up-down" is that notes and rests can either start on "down" or they can start on "up." Most of the time, they start on "down," but not always.

A little later you will learn why it's important for your child to think of *one beat* as having two parts ("down" and "up"). For now, just tell him that ONE BEAT = "DOWN" + UP" or "UP + DOWN."

WHOLE NOTES AND WHOLE RESTS

A *whole note* or *whole rest* lasts four *beats*. To count either one, your child should tap his foot "down-up" four times, or "up-down" four times. The full pattern would be "down-up, down-up, down-up, down-up" or "up-down, up-down, up-down, up-down."

Figure 20 shows a whole note and a whole rest and how they are counted. Notice that a whole note looks like a squashed donut, and a whole rest looks like it is hanging from the line. (Actually, the whole rest hangs from the fourth line up from the bottom.) Notice, too, that I've substituted "down-up arrows" for the "down-up feet." The "down" arrow stands for a "down" foot tap, the "up" arrow for when the foot comes "up." We will use the arrows from now on instead of drawing little feet.

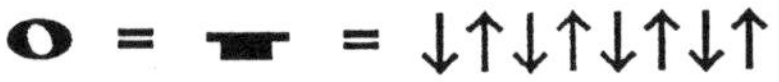

o = ▬ = ↓↑↓↑↓↑↓↑

Figure 20

Important rule: Every "down" is followed by an "up" (and vice versa). You never have two "downs" together or two "ups" together. This follows an important law of physics that states: "What goes 'down' must come 'up'." At least I think it's a law of physics.

Exercise 3:3—Have your child draw several whole notes and whole rests on staff paper. Make sure he makes his whole notes look like slightly squashed donuts, and that he hangs the whole rest from the fourth line. Have your child draw in "down-up" arrows for his notes and rests. He can start some of them on "up" and draw in "up-down" arrows if he likes. There should be four sets of "down-up" or "up-down" arrows for each note or rest. Refer to Figure 20 for help.

Exercise 3:4—Now have your child practice the "down-up" (or "up-down") foot tap for each of his whole notes and whole rests. Do not have your child count by saying "1 and, 2 and, etc.," when he does the "down-up" foot tap. He has to keep track of the number of "down-ups" (or "up-downs") in his head.

To reinforce the idea that a whole note sounds continuously for four beats, have your child sing his whole notes on the syllable "ta," while tapping his foot "down-up" (or "up-down") four times for each note.

I like using "ta" instead of "la" because that gives a definite "start" to the note and makes it easier to coordinate the beginning of the note and the "down" part of the foot tap.

Naturally, there is no sound for rests—just four "down-ups" or "up-downs."

Keep "Pitch" and "Rhythm" Separate

When singing rhythms, it doesn't matter what note your child sings, or if he sings a "note" at all. The idea is that the sound must be continuous. Since your child is learning to read "notes" and "rhythms" at the same time, he might choose to write specific "notes" for his "rhythm" exercises. That's fine; just don't insist on the right pitch when you are teaching rhythm. Keep the two elements separate when you teach them. Let the integration occur naturally with your child.

HALF NOTES AND HALF RESTS

A *half note* or *half rest* lasts two beats (Figure 21).

$$ \quad \mathbf{\downarrow} = \mathbf{\rho} = \mathbf{\_\!\_\!\_} = \downarrow\uparrow\downarrow\uparrow $$

Figure 21

The note part of a half note looks like a whole note—it just has a stem attached to it. The stem can go up or down. Typically, if the note is above the middle line of the staff, the stem goes down. If the note is below the middle line, the stem goes up. Notes on the middle line can go either way—but usually go whichever way most of the notes on that line go.

Notice that the stem is on the right side of the note when it goes up and on the left side of the note when it goes down. A half rest sits on the third line up from the bottom of the staff. The whole rest and half rest both have the same shape—the difference has to do with which line they touch.

Exercise 3:5—Have your child draw several half notes and half rests. As with Exercise 3:3, make sure he draws them accurately. Also have him draw in "down-up" or "up-down" arrows under each half note and half rest. Check Figure 21 if you need help.

Exercise 3:6—Have your child practice the foot tap while singing his half notes on "ta." As before, with the half rests, he taps his foot but doesn't "sing" anything.

QUARTER NOTES AND QUARTER RESTS

A *quarter note* or *quarter rest* lasts one beat (Figure 22). The rules for stem direction and placement on a quarter note are the same as for a half note.

Several years ago one of my students told me a quarter rest looked like a "snake in a blender." I liked that description and use it to this day. I don't bring this up for any particular reason, except perhaps to point out that my girlfriend from Chapter 2 isn't the only living creature that resembles a musical symbol.

♩ = 𝄽 = ⸮ = ↓↑ or ↑↓

Figure 22

Exercise 3:7—Ask your child to draw several quarter notes and quarter rests like those shown in Figure 22. As before, have him draw in the arrows. (One "down-up" or "up-down" for each quarter note or quarter rest.) Make sure his quarter rests are the "non-venomous" type. No sense asking for trouble.

Exercise 3:8—Have your child practice the foot tap while singing his quarter notes on "ta." As before, quarter rests get a foot tap, but no sound.

EIGHTH NOTES AND EIGHTH RESTS

An *eighth note* or *eighth rest* lasts one-half beat (Figure 23a). The eighth note looks like a quarter note with a "flag-shaped thing" attached to it. In musical terms, the "flag-shaped" thing is called—a *flag*. The eighth rest looks sort of like the number "7."

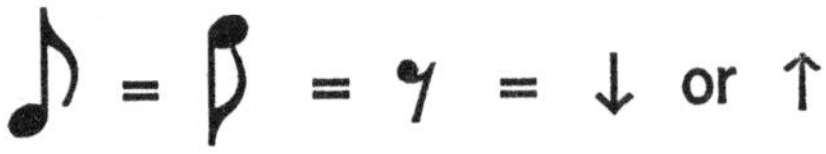

♪ = 𝄾 = ↓ or ↑

Figure 23a

Two Ways to Write Eighth Notes

When you have two or more eighth notes side by side, you can join their flags together (Figure 23b). Music is written both ways—it's really up to the person doing the writing—and it is usually done whichever way is easiest to read.

Figure 23b

Exercise 3:9—Have your child draw several eighth notes and eighth rests. Make sure he remembers those "flag-shaped things." (He can join the flags together or not. It doesn't matter.) This time when he draws in the down-up arrows, he will draw a "down" arrow under the first eighth note or eighth rest, and an "up" arrow under the next. The arrows alternate, "down," "up," etc. (Reminder: You never have two "down" arrows side by side or two "up" arrows side by side.)

Exercise 3:10—Have your child practice the "down-up" foot tap while singing his eighth notes on "ta." The first eighth note or rest gets "down"; the second one gets "up." This is the first time a note gets less than a whole beat or "down-up." With eighth notes, each "down" gets "ta" and each "up" gets "ta."

Counting the "down" and "up" parts of a beat separately is called *subdividing the beat*. Being able to subdivide the beat is critical to learning how to count rhythms in music; this is why I like the "down-up" foot tap. It forces subdivision from the beginning. By the time your child gets to eighth notes, he should be pretty good at it.

SIXTEENTH NOTES AND SIXTEENTH RESTS

Now, things start to get a little tricky! *Sixteenth notes* and *sixteenth rests* only last "one-fourth" of a beat. That's only half of a "down" or half of an "up." How, you may well ask, can we possibly count that?

Simple. We put two sixteenth notes or rests on every "down" and two on every "up." In professional music education circles we call this "TWO ON THE DOWN AND TWO ON THE UP." (At least that's what we call it in the circle I belong to.)

Notice in Figure 24a that a sixteenth note looks just like an eighth note with a spare flag. (A sixteenth rest looks like an eighth rest with a spare flag too.)

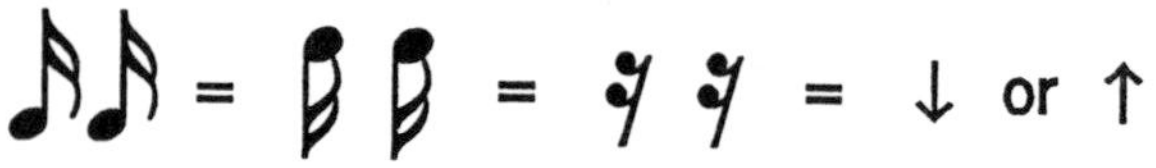

Figure 24a

Two Ways to Write Sixteenth Notes

Just as with eighth notes, you can join the flags of adjacent sixteenth notes together (Figure 24b).

Figure 24b

Exercise 3:11—Have your child draw several sixteenth notes and sixteenth rests and write in the "down-up" arrows. Make sure he doesn't forget to "double" the flags. As with eighth notes, he can join the flags together if he wants. Whichever way he does it, make sure he does "TWO ON THE DOWN AND TWO ON THE UP." (I'd hate to have to take a bad report back to the "circle.")

Exercise 3:12—Have your child practice the "down-up" foot tap while singing his sixteenth notes on "ta." Notice that the first two notes get "down," while the second two get "up." This means that your child will sing "ta-ta" for each "down" and "ta-ta" for each "up."

Another way to get the rhythm of sixteenth notes is to have your child say the phrase "Mississippi Mud," while tapping his foot. Try it. Have your child say, "Mis-sis-sip-pi Mud." "Mississippi" should sound like four sixteenth notes, "Mud" should sound like one.

BAR LINES AND MEASURES

To make it easier to keep track of the beats, vertical lines (called *bar lines*) divide the staff into *measures*. Each *measure* contains the same number of beats. In order to keep things simple, each measure will contain four beats. In regular music, the number of beats per measure is usually four, three, or two. Sometimes it's another number, but we'll have more on this in the section on Time Signatures. Figure 25 shows examples of bar lines and measures. The end of a piece of music is marked with a *double bar line*.

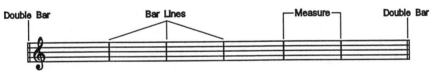

Figure 25

SYNCOPATION

From the beginning I have said notes and rests can start on "down" or they can start on "up." When a note starts on "up," that's called *syncopation*. (Actually, *syncopation* refers to any rhythm that places the emphasis on a normally "weak" beat, but for our purposes, syncopation occurs when a note starts on "up.")

Figure 26a and b shows two examples of syncopation. Notice that the first note or rest in each measure (after a bar line) starts on "down." No matter what—even with syncopation—the first note or rest in a measure starts on "down."

Figures 26a and 26b

Figure 26a starts with an eighth note, which gets "down." The next note is a quarter note. Since "up" always follows "down," the quarter note starts on "up," and is counted "up-down." Figure 26b shows the same rhythm, this time with an eighth rest at the beginning.

If you add up the note values for both measures in Figure 26a and b, you come up with a total of four beats per measure.

Whether a note or rest starts on "down" or "up" depends on where it comes in the measure. As stated earlier, however, the first note or rest in a measure starts with a "down" arrow. This is one rule that won't change.

Teach this rule to your child: THE FIRST NOTE OR REST IN A MEASURE ALWAYS STARTS ON "DOWN."

Exercise 3:13—Ask your child to draw bar lines on staff paper to create several measures, then have him fill these measures with notes and rests. Each measure must contain exactly four beats. No more. No less. To make sure he gets the right number of beats in each measure, have him draw in the arrows for each note or rest. (In order to end up with four beats, each measure should have a total of four "down" arrows and four "up" arrows.)

Remember: The first note or rest in every measure starts on "down." Also, remember that the arrows alternate. You can't have two "downs" or two "ups" together.

Exercise 3:14 — Have your child sing his measures on "ta" while he taps his foot.

TIES

If we draw lines connecting two or more notes of the same pitch together, we add up the value of those notes and make a new note that lasts as long as the combined number of beats of both notes (Figure 27).

Figure 27

The line connecting these notes is called a *tie*. Notice that notes that are tied together are the same pitch—that is, they are all the same line or space. A line drawn between notes of different pitch is called a *slur*. (More about "slurs" in the next chapter.)

Even with ties, the number of beats in each measure stays the same. What is different is that we can make our ties go across the bar line to make longer notes than we could have if we had to stay within the measure.

Notice that the tie in Figure 27 creates a note that lasts 4 beats plus 2 beats, or 6 beats total.

Figure 28 shows some other combinations of tied notes. By the way, rests are not tied together. There's no reason to tie them together because silence is silence no matter how you count it.

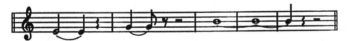

Figure 28

Exercise 3:15—Have your child draw several different combinations of tied notes and write in the "down-up arrows" and beats below. Even though the "tie" can cross over a bar line and make a note that lasts longer, each measure by itself must have exactly four beats in it.

Ask your child to tell you how long (how many beats) his "tied" notes last. Make sure he understands that this is "continuous" sound. Have him tap his foot and sing "ta" for each of his tied notes.

DOTTED NOTES

A small "dot" after a note or rest makes it last half again as long as it would normally. For example, a half note, which normally lasts for two beats, lasts for three beats with a dot after it (Figure 29).

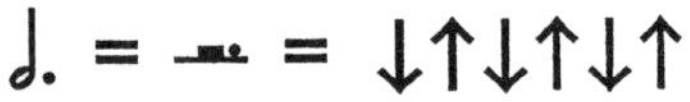

♩. = ▬▪ = ↓↑↓↑↓↑

Figure 29

Figure 30 shows a dotted quarter note and rest and how they are counted.

♩. = ♪. = ↓↑↓ or ↑↓↑

Figure 30

Exercise 3:16 — Have your child tap his foot and count the notes and rests in Figures 29 and 30. Notice that the dotted half note gets "down-up, down-up, down-up," and the dotted quarter note gets "down-up, down."

DOTTED-EIGHTH SIXTEENTH NOTE RHYTHM —A SPECIAL CASE

The dotted eighth note is a difficult rhythm to count and will require patience on your part to teach. One thing that helps is that a dotted eighth note is almost always followed by a sixteenth note. Hence the term *dotted-eighth sixteenth*.

Remember we said a dot adds half a note's regular value to it? An eighth note gets $1/2$ beat. Half of $1/2$ is $1/4$. Therefore, a dotted eighth note gets $3/4$'s of a beat ($1/2 = 2/4 + 1/4 = 3/4$). After this little exercise, I hope you can see how learning to read music can enhance learning in other subject areas such as math!

The problem is, it's impossible to count that rhythm using a "down-up" foot tap. Three-fourths of a beat is more than "down" and less than "down-up." (Actually, it's all the way "down" and halfway back "up.")

Figure 31 shows a measure with four dotted-eighth sixteenth rhythms. Notice that the sixteenth note comes just after the "up." If you say "uh" right after "up" and before your foot goes back down, you will probably come pretty close to this rhythm. Try it. Say: "Down-up-uh, down-up-uh, etc." To sound out the rhythm, try clapping on "down" and "uh." In Figure 31 the places to clap are marked with an "X."

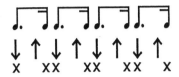

Figure 31

Another way to count the dotted-eighth sixteenth rhythm is to say "Play to-day." The way most people say "Play to-day" (with the word "play" long and the first syllable of the word "today" short) is close to a dotted-eighth sixteenth note rhythm.

Exercise 3:17—Have your child start a steady "down-up" foot tap, then clap the dotted-eighth sixteenth note rhythm in Figure 31. Then try "saying" the rhythm using the phrase "Play to-day." If one method seems to work better for your child than another, don't feel obligated to use both. The important thing is for your child to understand that the dotted eighth note is three times as long as the sixteenth note that usually follows it, and that the entire dotted-eighth sixteenth note rhythm takes place within one "down-up" foot tap.

TIME SIGNATURES

This is the part where I "fess up" and explain why a whole note doesn't always get four beats and why a measure doesn't always contain four beats.

At the beginning of all regular music you will find two numbers, one above the other. These sets of numbers are *time signatures*.

The top number in the time signature tells how many beats

there are in a measure. The bottom number tells what kind of note gets *one* beat.

In Figure 32 the top number—4—tells us that every measure in this piece of music will contain four beats. The bottom number —also 4—tells us that a *quarter* note (4 stands for quarter note) gets one beat.

Figure 32

But what if the top number isn't a "4"?

Figures 33a, 33b, 33c

The top number in Figure 33a tells us there are two beats in every measure. Figure 33b shows three beats to a measure; and Figure 33c indicates five beats to a measure. In all three cases, the bottom number is four, so a quarter note still gets one beat.

The largest note that will fit in a measure of 2/4 time is a half note (2 beats); the largest note that will fit in a measure of 3/4 time is a dotted-half note (3 beats); and the largest note that will fit in a 5/4 measure is a whole note tied to a quarter note (5 beats).

OK. So what if the bottom number isn't a 4?

Figures 34a, 34b, 34c

The bottom number in Figure 34a tells us an eighth note gets a beat. (The number "8" stands for eighth note.) The top number (4) tells us that there are four beats in a measure. Therefore in 4/8 time, there are four eighth notes (or equivalent) in a measure.

Figure 34b indicates that a half note gets a beat. The top number (4) tells us that each measure contains the equivalent of four half notes. In Figure 34c, a sixteenth note gets a beat, and there is the equivalent of four sixteenth notes in each measure.

Remember: The top number of the time signature tells *how many beats* in a measure, and the bottom number tells *what kind of note* gets a beat.

There are also two time signatures that don't involve numbers. They are shown in Figure 35a and b.

Figures 35a and 35b

Figure 35a is called "Common Time." It is the same as "4/4 time." Figure 35b is called "Cut Time," and it is the same as "2/2 time." (Two beats per measure; a half note gets a beat.)

Once you know which kind of note gets a beat, figuring out how many beats the other notes get is easy. Figure 36 shows how.

$$\circ = \,\downarrow\!\downarrow \qquad \downarrow = \,\downarrow\!\downarrow \qquad \downarrow = \,\flat\!\flat \qquad \flat = \,\flat\!\flat$$

Figure 36

All you have to do is determine which kind of note gets a beat and either multiply or divide to figure out what the other notes get. For example, with 2/8 time, an eighth note gets a beat. Therefore, since a quarter note equals two eighth notes, a quarter note gets two beats. Conversely, it takes two sixteenth notes to equal an eighth note, so in 2/8 time, a sixteenth note gets half a beat.

Changing the "down-up" foot taps to fit the time signature is also easy. In the 2/8 example above, since an eighth note now gets a beat, it gets "down-up." A quarter note gets two beats, so it gets "down-up, down-up."

Exercise 3:18 — Go over Figures 32 through 36 with your child. Have him make up and draw some time signatures of his own on staff paper. The top number can be any number. The bottom number must be 4 (quarter note gets a beat); 2 (half note gets a beat); 8 (eighth note gets a beat); or 16 (sixteenth note gets a beat).

Ask your child to tell you how many beats there are in a measure for each of his time signatures and which kind of note gets a beat.

TO SUM UP

This chapter has outlined the basic components of reading rhythm. While it may seem basic, it's a lot of information to process. If your child learns the material in Chapters 2 and 3, he will be well on his way to independent music reading.

Hey, look who's back just in time to carry us off to Chapter 4! Hi there, little feet! What's up? (Or down.) Oh, *you* are!

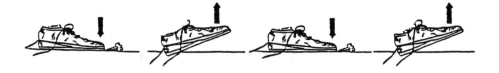

4.
MUSIC READING: OTHER MUSICAL SIGNS

In this chapter we tie up the loose ends regarding music reading. This chapter contains some other musical signs your child will need to understand in order to be able to interpret music as the composer intended.

There are no exercises in this chapter. You can teach these signs to your child by going over them and having him memorize the names and meanings, or you can use this chapter as a reference to look up unfamiliar signs when they come up in music.

MUSICAL SHORTHAND

Music is filled with abbreviations. They are mainly used to save space but often serve to make the music easier to read. Your child will come across many musical abbreviations, so he should be able to recognize them and know how they work.

Repeat Sign

A *repeat* sign is a *double bar* with two dots:

‖: :‖

Figure 37

A repeat sign tells us to return to a similar sign facing the other way around or, if there is no other sign, to go back to the beginning of the piece of music and play or sing it again. Figure 38a shows a repeat sign within a song; Figure 38b shows one in which we return to the beginning of the music.

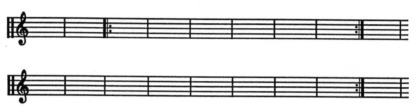

Figures 38a and 38b

Repeat Measure

Figure 39 shows a *repeat measure* sign. This means to repeat the preceding measure.

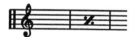

Figure 39

If the repeat measure sign is over a bar line, it means to repeat the *two* previous measures (Figure 40).

Figure 40

Sometimes there is a number above a repeat measure sign. That means to repeat as many of the preceding measures as the number indicates. Figure 41 indicates that the previous four measures are to be repeated.

Figure 41

Repeated Rests

If a rest is to last longer than one measure (whole rest), a sign like the one shown in Figure 42 is used. The number above the sign tells how many measures of rest there are.

Figure 42

First and Second Endings

First and *second endings* provide a way to repeat a section of music yet put a different ending on it the second time through. Figure 43 shows how the "second" ending simply takes the place of the "first" ending on the repeat.

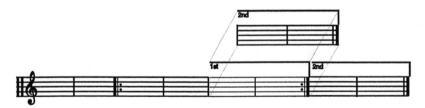

Figure 43

D.C. Al Fine

D.C. is an abbreviation for the Italian words *da capo*, which means "go back to the beginning." *D.C. al fine* means to go back to the beginning and play to the *fine* (fee-nay) or "end."

Figure 44

D.S. Al Fine

D.S. is an abbreviation for *dal segno*, which means: "go back to the sign." *Al fine*, just as before, means to play or sing to the "end." Figure 45 shows how D.S. al fine works.

Figure 45

D.S. Al Coda

D.S. al coda means to go back to the sign and play or sing from there to the *coda sign*, which, I think, looks like a "submarine periscope." When you get to the "periscope," you "dive" to the coda. The coda is a special ending—sort of the composer's last word. Figure 46 shows how D.S. al coda works.

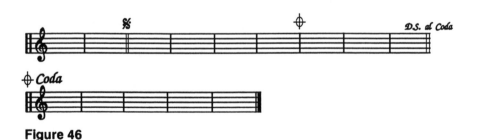

Figure 46

TEMPO

Tempo refers to how fast or slow the music is to be played or sung. An indication of the speed of the music (tempo) is normally given at the beginning of the music in English or Italian. Here are some common tempo indicators in both languages.

English

Tempo indications in English are fairly easy to understand. Here are some common English terms from slowest to fastest:

Slowest	Very Slowly
	Slow
	Steady
	March Time
	Moderate (medium)
	Brightly
	Lively
	Rather Fast
Fastest	Very Fast

Italian

Here are some of the more common Italian words used to indicate tempo, from slowest to fastest. (Since the words are in Italian, I have also included their meanings.)

Slowest	Lento or Largo	Very Slow
	Adagio	Slow, Leisurely
	Andante	At "walking pace"
	Moderato	Medium
	Allegro	Fast
	Vivace	Lively
	Presto	Very Fast
Fastest	Molto	Very (i.e, Molto Allegro = Very Fast)

Metronome Marking

When words are used to indicate tempo, as in the above examples, these words don't tell us *exactly* how fast to play or sing the music. These are *relative* terms. The tempo or speed of the music depends on our interpretation of just what is meant by "Very Slowly" or "Allegro" or "Presto."

Another and more accurate way of indicating tempo is to use a metronome marking (mm); an indication of how many beats there are per minute. For example, mm ♩ = 120 means there should be 120 quarter notes per minute. All we have to do is set a clock-like instrument called a "metronome" to 120, and the metronome clicks at the proper speed to tell us the tempo. Then, try to keep up!

Change of Tempo

Often the composer wants the music to become slower or get faster for dramatic effect. The following Italian words and signs are used to indicate a change in the tempo:

Rallentando (Rall.) or *Ritardando* (Ritard.) means to slow down gradually. *Accelerando* (Accel.) means to speed up gradually. *A tempo* means to go back to the original tempo or speed.

Hold (Fermata)

A *hold* sign is written over a note or rest and tells us that the note or rest is to be held out longer than normal. The Italian word for "hold" is *fermata*. The actual length of the "hold" is left up to the performer or the conductor. Often a hold is found on the last note of a piece of music (Figure 47).

Figure 47

DYNAMICS

Another way in which the composer varies music is to indicate different levels of loudness, called *dynamics*.

Here are some common Italian indicators of loudness and softness from softest to loudest:

Softest	ppp	Pianississimo	As soft as possible
	pp	Pianissimo	Very soft
	p	Piano	Soft

mp	Mezzo Piano	Moderately soft
m	Mezzo	Medium
mf	Mezzo Forte	Moderately loud
f	Forte	Loud
ff	Fortissimo	Very loud
Loudest fff	Fortississimo	As loud as possible

Change of Dynamics

Just as tempo can be changed for effect, so can dynamics. Here are the two most common terms (and signs) used to indicate a change in dynamics.

Cres. or <	Crescendo	Gradually get louder
Dim. or >	Diminuendo	Gradually get softer

MISCELLANEOUS SIGNS

Here are a few miscellaneous signs that don't seem to fit in anywhere else.

Slur

Remember the *tie*, the curved line that links notes of the same pitch together to create a longer note? A curved line over two or more notes of *different* pitch is called a *slur*. This means the notes should be played or sung *smoothly*. Slurs are also used to mark musical phrases, "bowing" for stringed instruments, and the way words fit into songs.

Figure 48

Staccato

A dot *above* or *below* a note means it should be *staccato* — played or sung with a space between the note and its neighbor. Be careful that your child doesn't confuse a dot above or below a note with one beside it. A dot beside a note makes it one and a half times longer; a dot above or below means to "space" the note. See Figure 49.

Figure 49

Accent

An *accent* above or below a note means the note should be played or sung *strongly*, but not *spaced* like staccato. There are two main types of accents, regular and extra-crispy. Whoops, I mean regular and extra-strong.

Figure 50

Tenuto

Tenuto means the note so marked should be played or sung firmly—for its full value. This marking is often used to make sure the performer doesn't play or sing the notes too short. (Some composers can't help being worrywarts.)

Figure 51

TRIPLETS

Triplets are groups of three notes fitted into the time of two. Triplets must be played or sung evenly. Each note must get the same amount of time. There are two main kinds of triplets, *eighth note triplets* and *quarter note triplets*. (Actually, you can have triplets made of any three notes of the same kind, but these two are the most common.)

Eighth Note Triplets

With eighth note triplets, three eighth notes must be played in the time it normally takes to play two. A little trick that sometimes help with counting triplets is to say the word BEAU-TI-FUL as evenly and smoothly as possible during one "down-up" foot tap. It's best to start the "down-up" foot tap going first, then add the word "beau-ti-ful." Figure 52 shows how this works.

Figure 52

Quarter Note Triplets

Quarter note triplets follow the same principle, but the notes are longer. You can use the word BEAU-TI-FUL for quarter note triplets also. Just make it last two "down-up" foot taps (Figure 53).

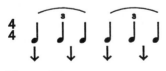

Figure 53

6/8 TIME SIGNATURE—TWO WAYS TO COUNT IT

There are two ways 6/8 time can be counted. For one of them, you simply follow the standard formula for time signatures. The top number (6) tells us there are six beats per measure. The bottom number (8) tells us the eighth note gets a beat. When we tap our foot, we tap it "down-up" six times (once for each eighth note).

Figure 54   **Figure 55**

The other way to count 6/8 time is in "two" (two beats per measure). We see 6/8 counted in two mostly for fast marches. When 6/8 time is counted in two, the "foot tap" consists of "Down-2-3, Down-2-3." In other words, we don't pay any attention to the "up" part of the beat. Naturally the foot has to come back up before it can go down again, we just don't care when it happens.

When learning a piece of music that is written in 6/8 time intended to be taken in "two," it is a good idea to start by taking it in "six." After learning the counting and note values, your child can then speed up the foot-tap and take it in "two."

TO SUM UP

Chapters 2, 3, and 4 have presented a *basic* guide to reading music. There are other kinds of notes and rests and other musical symbols that are used in written music, but with the background found in these three chapters, your child should be able to read and understand most of the music he comes across.

5.

MAKING MUSIC

It would be pointless for your child to learn to read music if he never actually made music. That is why this chapter on making music was written.

As important as it is for your child to learn to read music, it's even more important for your child to learn to make music. Your child can make music by singing or by playing an instrument. I believe all children should do both.

SINGING

Singing involves training the voice to match pitch or sing on-key with the right notes and rhythms. Most parents, whether musically trained or not, can tell when their child sings off-key. Fortunately, learning to sing the right notes and rhythms is a skill any child can learn—provided he gets enough practice and repetition.

The younger your child is when singing begins, the better, but if you choose appropriate songs, records, or tapes and encourage your child to sing along with them, a child of any age can learn to sing.

"Hold the phone, Marge! Did the man just say any child can learn to sing? Surely, he doesn't mean my little Elwood! Poor little 'tone-deaf' Elwood is just like his father. He couldn't carry a tune in a bucket! Shoot, he couldn't carry a tune in a dump truck! Why, he couldn't carry a tune in a . . ."

All right, already! You made your point! The fact is, except where there is an organic hearing deficiency, any child can learn to match pitch and sing in tune. Some children have a limited range of only a few notes—others will have more—but with enough listening and repetition, your child can learn to sing.

Most young children, in fact, love to sing, and you should reinforce your child's natural desire to vocalize by creating as many opportunities for singing as possible.

Children's singing should, for the most part, be accompanied by an instrument (piano, guitar, etc.), to help reinforce matching pitch and to establish a sense of tonality (key).

If you play piano or guitar, there are a number of excellent songbooks that contain music appropriate for children of all ages. If you do not play an instrument, you can encourage your child to sing through the use of sing-along records and tapes.

Your child's elementary general music classes include lots of singing, and the teacher will probably be happy to recommend commercially available songbooks or "sing-along" records and tapes the teacher uses and likes. Many music teachers use the *Hap Palmer* series of books and cassettes, as well as those of popular Disney Channel star Raffi. The award-winning *Ella Jenkins* series emphasizes movement to music and the *Silly Song Book* contains fifty-five humorous tunes that most youngsters love to sing.

There are many others. Before you buy, find out if your public library has any of these materials, so you can try them out and choose the ones that seem most appropriate for your child. For those you want to own, check with your local music, book, or record store—or refer to one of the sources listed in Chapter 8.

Older students (junior high and high school age) who want "sing-along" materials might enjoy a series called *Pocket Songs—You Sing the Hits!* Available on cassette tape and CD, *Pocket Songs* allows the singer to remove the vocals and sing along with full back-up band accompaniment. *Pocket Songs* offers more than 4,000 popular songs ranging in style from country and western to pop and rock, Broadway, blues, and even old standards.

HELPING YOUR CHILD LEARN TO SING

Here are some ways you can take an active role in encouraging your child to express himself or herself in song.

Learn the Songs Yourself

If you don't play an instrument, listen to the "sing-along" records or tapes until you know the words and melody to the songs your child will sing. Even if you don't fancy yourself much of a singer, try singing along. You might be surprised at how easy it is. Your child will be more willing to sing if you, as the parent music teacher, help set the "tone."

Memorize the Words

Teach your child to recite the song verses rhythmically—like a poem. This will help him to develop memory skills. Your child will find it easier to learn the melody if learning the words is already accomplished.

Repetition

Play the song (or record) several times before trying to get your child to sing. The more your child hears the song, the better he will learn it. The Suzuki Talent Education program, discussed later in this chapter, compares learning to sing or play an instrument to learning spoken language. According to Suzuki, just as a child learns to speak his native tongue by imitation and repetition, so too can he learn to play or sing music.

Learning by repetition and imitation is called "rote learning." It's the basis for early singing in elementary general music programs—especially those that use the Kodaly system. As your child gets older and learns how to read music, he should be able to sing independently, but in the beginning he needs to "hear" music in order to "make" music.

Listen

After a few times of listening and singing together, let your child "sing" to you. This will give you an opportunity to evaluate your child's progress, determine whether the words and melody have been learned, etc.

If you have a tape recorder, record your child singing and let him listen to himself to evaluate his own progress. Don't do this, however, until your child sings with enough confidence that you are convinced he won't be discouraged when he listens to his own voice.

Use Printed Music

If you play an instrument, encourage your child to follow along in the music as you play. Young children develop "pre-reading" skills by following along while a parent reads stories to them. The same process can be true with music. Even for very young children who have not learned to read music notation, there is value in beginning to set the idea that the "little black dots" represent musical sounds. If you are using records or tapes, try to get those that include at least a melody line along with the words, and help your child follow along while you point to the words and notes.

Praise

Be quick to praise any success your child has — getting the words right, singing the tune correctly, anything. In fact, you should find reasons to praise your child every single time he sings. If the only thing he gets right are a few of the words, then praise that! Nothing destroys a child's confidence and willingness to sing faster than the feeling that he is not successful.

Singing Games

Singing games provide your child with the opportunity to sing as well as move rhythmically or act out a story. Many singing games are taught in general music classes. Your child will probably want to show new games to you as they are taught in school. Encourage your child to "teach" the games to you and practice them at home.

There are also a number of excellent books that include singing games you can teach your child at home. As with the materials listed above, check at local stores or with one of the sources listed in Chapter 8.

Piano Lessons

To be able to sit down at the piano and accompany yourself (and your friends) as you sing is, perhaps, the quintessential musical experience. Providing your child with piano lessons while encouraging and nurturing his singing skills will give him pleasure for the rest of his life.

SINGING GROUPS

Singing by yourself can be rewarding, but singing in a group is FUN! Your child will have numerous opportunities to join singing groups during his school years. I hope you will encourage him to take advantage of as many of these opportunities as possible.

Elementary Grades

Many grade schools have a choir—often directed by the general music teacher. Sometimes this group meets after school, sometimes during the school day. Typically, grade school choirs emphasize "group singing for fun" as well as teaching fundamentals and a few vocal techniques. The choir is frequently featured on school music programs, and sometimes travels to nursing homes and other community centers to perform.

Most churches have children's choirs. Many communities sponsor a youth choir as part of the city recreation program. Community-sponsored youth choirs sometimes go on annual trips or tours to other cities, or even have "exchange" programs with other community-sponsored youth singing groups.

Middle School and Junior High

Middle school and junior high school choirs, when taught by a skilled teacher who knows how to deal with the adolescent changing voice, can be a rewarding experience for your child.

Boys at this age level are particularly unwilling to sing because their voices are going through so many changes—they sound like Darth Vader one minute, Princess Leia the next. A good middle school or junior high choir director can help your child through this traumatic period and even provide a sense of self-confidence through proper voice training.

High School

Most high schools offer a number of singing opportunities for older students, including concert choir, madrigal groups, Broadway-style musical productions, and the choral version of the jazz band, the show choir. Some of these ensembles are open only through audition; others, any student can join.

Encourage your child to join a singing group in his school or in the community. Group singing can be a very rewarding musical experience, and since the instrument (the voice) is built in, singing is one of the least expensive ways of all to make music.

PLAYING AN INSTRUMENT

I believe every child should learn to play at least one musical instrument—the piano.

Why, you ask? Simple. Have you ever met anyone who said: "I'm really glad I never learned to play the piano?" I haven't. I have met many people who told me they wish they had learned how when they were younger. In many cases, they didn't even try because they or their parents didn't think they had the talent. That's too bad, because the truth is, just as any child can learn to sing, any child can learn to play the piano. Some will be better at it than others, but they can all learn enough to enjoy making music for the rest of their lives.

THE PIANO—A GOOD PLACE TO START

Teaching music reading is so much more meaningful when your child can "hear" as well as "see" the notes. That's why I hope you have (or will get) a piano for your child.

Your child could start Suzuki piano lessons as early as age three or four. Typically, children start on piano in the third grade (age eight). This doesn't mean your fifth-grader is too old to start piano lessons. On the contrary, it's never too late to start learning to play piano. In fact, if you buy your child a piano and don't know how to play yourself, I suggest you sign up for lessons too!

Some elementary general music classes and a few middle school or junior high general music classes include class instruction on piano or keyboard, but most do not. Even when class instruction is offered, it cannot do a better job than private lessons.

Acoustic Piano

An acoustic piano is a "regular" piano—one that doesn't require electricity, an amplifier, or a computer chip in order to make music.

A standard acoustic piano has eighty-eight keys. Most people get either a spinet (36 to 38 inches high), a console piano (40 to 42 inches high), or a studio piano (44 to 46 inches high). These are all "vertical" or "upright" pianos, so named because the strings run vertically rather than horizontally as in a grand piano. Few people invest in a grand piano. For one thing, grand pianos take up a lot of space and for another, a typical grand piano costs approximately as much as a beachfront house in Malibu.

The Piano Book by Larry Fine is an excellent guide to buying a new or used piano. It covers every aspect of piano buying from selection to service and includes an evaluation of many different pianos by brand name.

Digital Pianos

Digital pianos have the look and feel of regular acoustic pianos. Many sound so much like an acoustic piano that even experts have trouble telling the difference.

Digital pianos are expensive (typically $2,500 or more for a basic model), but unlike an acoustic piano, they never need tuning. Also, most digital pianos have several "voices" or instrument sounds built in and can be connected to a computer through a MIDI interface and used with software to teach your child music theory or to allow him to "perform" music and print it out on a printer.

Electronic Keyboards, Synthesizers, and MIDI

Like many music teachers, I'm partial to the acoustic piano, but an inexpensive electronic keyboard is fine, especially for learning how to read music. I would like to admonish you to get a keyboard with *full-size* keys, though. By that I mean the keys should be the same size as regular piano keys. Electronic keyboards typically have about forty-nine keys—a little more than half the number of keys on a full piano keyboard.

Some electronic keyboards also include a MIDI input and output and, like digital pianos, can be hooked up to a computer for use with music-related software.

Miracle Piano Teaching System

If your child already has the Nintendo® Video Game System and you are thinking about getting an electronic keyboard, you may want to consider the Miracle Piano Teaching System, which is discussed more fully in Chapter 8. The Miracle System includes an electronic keyboard and Nintendo® software that helps drill your child on basic keyboard and music reading skills.

The Miracle System won't take the place of a "real" teacher, but it might motivate your child to practice piano and want to learn from a real teacher. I wouldn't recommend a Miracle Piano Teaching System instead of a piano, but I think it has merit as a way to motivate children to learn keyboard skills.

GUITAR—ACOUSTIC OR ELECTRIC?

Guitars come in two basic types—acoustic and electric. The distinction between the two is contained in their names. Acoustic guitars make their sound "acoustically," without amplification; electric guitars rely on an electric impulse that goes through an amplifier.

If your child wants to learn to play guitar, I recommend he start on an acoustic (non-electric) model. For one thing, a student-line acoustic guitar is self-contained and can be bought for less than $200. An electric guitar usually costs about $300 or more and requires an amplifier (another $200 or so).

If you spend five or six hundred dollars on an electric guitar and amplifier, and your child loses interest or only uses the instrument to make "outer space" sound effects instead of practicing, you may find it difficult to support him later on in other music endeavors.

The fact is, many children love the idea of being able to play guitar, but when they realize it requires dedication and lots of practice to achieve proficiency, some lose their enthusiasm. Actually, most lose their enthusiasm.

In the long run, it's better to start with a relatively inexpensive acoustic guitar and provide private lessons until your child is able to decide for himself which type of guitar-playing he wants to do. The type of playing—classical, blues, country-western, rock, etc.—determines, to a large extent, the type of instrument he will want to own. Ask the school music teacher for recommendations regarding private guitar teachers.

Your child can begin learning to play guitar as early as eight or nine years old. Some children, if their hands are small, require a 3/4 size instrument at this age; others can play a full-size guitar. Your child's guitar teacher can advise you on the size instrument to get.

Some music stores rent guitars to students during the initial months of private instruction and will apply all or part of your rental to the eventual purchase of an instrument.

By the way, many junior high general music classes include some class instruction in guitar and provide an instrument. Just as with class piano or keyboard, this won't be enough for the truly interested child, but it might be enough if your child already plays the piano or a band or orchestra instrument.

ORCHESTRA

In school districts where there is an orchestra program, classes on stringed instruments (violin, viola, cello, and double bass) are usually offered beginning in the fourth or fifth grade.

Classes are taught by a specialist on stringed instruments—often the district orchestra director—and normally take place during the school day.

If your child's school has a string program, your child will probably bring home information about the program, including information on the availability of school-owned instruments. In some orchestra programs, the school provides an instrument at little or no cost to the parents; in others, the parent has to rent or buy an instrument from a music dealer.

BAND

Not all schools have an orchestra program, but almost every school has a band. Band usually begins in the fifth or sixth grade. Most beginners start on flute, clarinet, cornet (trumpet), trombone, saxophone, or percussion (snare drum and bells). Other instruments such as the oboe, bassoon, horn, euphonium (baritone horn), and tuba are sometimes played by beginners, but more often they are "switched to" during middle school or junior high.

As with the string program, your child will bring home information about the band program when he is eligible to join. Some schools provide beginner band instruments, but in most schools parents have to rent or buy an instrument from a local music dealer.

My book, *A Parent's Guide to Band and Orchestra* (Betterway Publications, 1991), provides a step-by-step guide to getting your child started in band or orchestra, buying or renting an instrument, and helping your child maintain his interest and develop as a member of the school music ensemble.

SUZUKI MUSIC CLASSES

A special approach to teaching violin (and more recently, piano) has been developed by Shinichi Suzuki of Japan. The system is called Talent Education and is based on Suzuki's philosophy that all children are capable of learning to make music in the same way they learn to speak—by imitation and repetition.

Children (along with their parents) attend Suzuki violin or piano classes as early as preschool age. Parent involvement is an important part of the Suzuki approach. Parents are expected to attend classes and help supervise practice at home.

Listening to music is also an important component of the Suzuki approach. All the music taught is available on tapes for parents to play at home so their child will learn to imitate the musical sounds he hears.

Suzuki classes aren't often offered in elementary schools, but because the Talent Education program is so widespread, most string and piano teachers are familiar with the Suzuki philosophy.

If you want to know more about the Suzuki program, check with your school strings teacher or call a local college or university. (University music teachers often know where the nearest Suzuki classes are.) Or write the Suzuki Association of the Americas listed in Appendix B.

HOME PRACTICE

No matter what instrument your child decides to play —including singing (the voice is also an instrument) — one of your principal roles as a parent-music teacher is to help supervise home practice. Simply put, your child will not succeed if you don't help. You must see to it that your child has a regular daily time for practice and that he sticks to a "practice system."

Each daily practice session can be broken down into three parts: warm-up, drill, and wrap-up.

Warm-Up

Whether vocalizing, playing long tones, or scales, every practice session should begin with a short warm-up period. It doesn't have to be long for youngsters. Two to five minutes is plenty.

Drill

After warm-up your child should go through an exercise or a song he intends to learn — once completely through, to identify problem spots—then back through to work on those places.

He should practice slowly and methodically, identifying areas that need attention and going over them until he can sing or play them four times without mistakes. The conclusion of the drill should include going back through the song or exercise again.

Drill can take anywhere from ten to fifteen minutes.

Wrap-Up

The wrap-up of each practice session should consist of playing or singing something your child has already learned. The idea here is to finish each practice session on a positive note. The wrap-up part of a practice session can last from three to five minutes.

Many parents believe it takes an hour or more a day of practice to master an instrument or learn to sing. This simply isn't true. If you add up the times above, you'll see that a practice session should last anywhere from fifteen to twenty-five minutes.

These times are good for elementary and junior high students. High school students (with longer assignments) probably need more practice—half an hour to forty-five minutes.

No child, however, needs to practice an hour every day. That's too much to ask of a youngster. Frankly, it's too much to ask of most adults!

PRIVATE LESSONS

Whether your child sings, plays an instrument, or does both, at some point the question of private lessons will come up. Guidelines for singers differ from those for instrumentalists.

Voice Lessons

Formal voice training shouldn't begin until your child has gone through puberty. A youngster's voice changes during adolescence; training the "changing voice" is very tricky. The net result of improper training can be permanent damage to the vocal cords.

After the voice matures, private or small group voice lessons provide one way for talented and motivated students to learn how to use their voices or to prepare for a professional singing career.

When it comes to training young voices (even after they have matured), care must be taken not to strain them or force them to sing too high or too low. For this reason, it's best to talk with the school vocal music teacher (choir director) before signing your child up for singing lessons. The vocal teacher will know which private teachers are skilled in dealing with young voices.

Instrumental Lessons

Instrumental private lessons can start any time, although with band and orchestra instruments, most children wait until junior high to begin private study.

For some instruments there is no choice. Piano and guitar lessons, for example, are not normally offered at school, so if your child wants to learn either of these instruments, you will have to sign him up for private lessons from the very beginning.

Your best source for advice on getting a private teacher—even for piano and guitar—is the school music teacher. In some communities, the local piano teachers' guild also offers a referral service to help match children up with piano teachers, based on the student's interest and the kind of piano playing he or she plans to do.

SPECIAL ABILITIES: PERFECT PITCH VS. RELATIVE PITCH

Some children seem to have an uncanny ability to sing or play almost any song "by ear." They only have to hear it once, and they can "remember" it. Once these children learn note names, they are able to "name notes" as they hear them. This ability is called *perfect pitch*.

Perfect pitch (also called *absolute pitch*) is the innate ability to name instantly and without fail any note struck on the piano or played on any instrument. It appears at a very early age and is very rare, even among professional musicians. (There are those who claim perfect pitch can be taught, but I'm not convinced.)

Perfect pitch, however, should no more be confused with "talent" than large muscles should be confused with "strength." It's what you *do* with what you *have* that determines talent, not what you have to begin with.

For example: Both Wagner and Tchaikovsky lacked perfect pitch, yet both managed to write some pretty catchy tunes. In fact, trained musicians develop what is known as *relative pitch* (the ability to name an interval in relation to a known pitch by remembering the interval). Some musicians get so good at it and develop such good *pitch memory* that it is hard to tell from perfect pitch.

It is common for people with perfect pitch to be driven up the wall when they hear others playing or singing slightly off-key. One of my fellow music teachers has perfect pitch, and I have seen her leave a performance because out-of-tune singing or playing gave her a headache. (She understands it's not the fault of the performers—they can't possibly hear what she hears.)

On the other hand, while accompanying our high school choir, the same music teacher became aware the choir had slipped down almost half a step in pitch during a number. She transposed the piano accompaniment to fit the new "key" the choir was singing in, thereby avoiding a "musical train wreck" between the piano and the voices at the end! (Had she not developed the "talent" to transpose the piano part, the "gift" of perfect pitch would simply have allowed her to know that a "train wreck" was about to occur!)

Think of a child with perfect pitch as having X-ray hearing. Maybe people with perfect pitch should be required to wear a cape with a big ear on it and spend at least one day a week helping rid the world of bad intonation. (Well, it's an idea.)

If your child shows any indication that he has perfect pitch, talk with the school music teacher. The teacher can test your child to determine whether he has perfect pitch or a highly-developed sense of relative pitch.

6.

LISTENING TO MUSIC

Your child's music education should include listening to music of a variety of styles and historical periods. This chapter provides some background so you can offer your child a broad palette of listening experiences.

You can use the information in this chapter to develop a "listening curriculum" for your child, or you can go through the "Musical Styles" section in the order presented. However you do it, your main goal should be to expose your child to as many different kinds of music as possible.

I have not identified specific records to listen to in this chapter, but instead offer a brief "starter" list of suggested compositions in many style categories.

If you want more specific suggestions on recordings to listen to, check out a book called *All Ears* by Jill Jarnow. This guide on how to use and choose recorded music for children contains a special section that profiles more than seventy-five artists and highlights over two hundred recordings appropriate for children.

THE PUBLIC LIBRARY

The best source of sound recordings is your local public library. You can borrow records, cassettes, and CDs at no charge.

Most libraries have a fairly extensive collection of sound recordings.

Many libraries catalog sound recordings using the Alpha-Numeric System for Classification of Recordings (ANSCR). Use the chart below to save time when looking for recorded materials.

If your library doesn't use ANSCR, ask the librarian to show you how to look up music according to classification or style.

ANSCR

A   Music Appreciation—History and Commentary
B   Operas: Complete and Highlights
C   Choral Music
D   Vocal Music
E   Orchestra Music:
        EA General Orchestral
        EB Ballet Music
        EC Concertos
        ES Symphonies
F   Chamber Music
G   Solo Instrumental Music:
        GG Guitar
        GO Organ
        GP Piano
        GS Stringed Instruments
        GV Violin
        GW Wind Instruments
        GX Percussion Instruments
H   Band Music
J   Electronic, Mechanical Music
K   Musical Shows and Operettas: Complete and Excerpts
L   Soundtrack Music: Motion Pictures and Television
M   Popular Music:
        MA Pop Music
        MC Country and Western Music
        MJ Jazz
        MR Rock, Rhythm, Blues, etc.
P   Folk and Ethnic Music: National
Q   International Folk and Ethnic Music

R   Holiday Music
S   Varieties and Humor
      (Comics, Monologues, Musical Satire, Comedy Acts, etc.)
T   Plays
U   Poetry
V   Prose
W   Documentary: History and Commentary
X   Instructional:
              (Diction, Languages, "How to ...", etc.)
Y   Sounds and Special Effects
Z   Children's Recordings:
              ZI Instructional
              ZM Music
              ZS Spoken

VIDEO TAPES

In addition to records, tapes, and CDs, many libraries have large collections of video tapes that can be incorporated into a listening program. Operas, operettas, musicals, and concerts especially lend themselves to this kind of format.

ACTIVE LISTENING

Most children, when they play a record or tape, do not *actively listen* to the music. Most adults, in fact, are the same way. We have become so accustomed to "background" music, we don't even think about the musical sounds that surround us every day. Active listening requires your child (and you) to listen for specific elements in the music, and then discuss them after the music ends.

To prepare your child to begin to listen to music actively, try this exercise. Give your child a piece of paper and a pencil and tell him to write down all the sounds he hears. These do not have to be musical sounds, but any sounds your child can identify, such as a dog barking, a car driving by, people talking, etc.

You and your child will probably both be surprised at the number and variety of sounds going on around you all the time.

Tell your child that, from now on, when he listens to music, he will also be listening for many different elements or "musical sounds." Only with music, you and he will decide ahead of time which elements to listen for.

Here are some guidelines you should use every time you and your child listen to music.

Pay Attention

You and your child must give your full attention to the music. Don't expect your child to listen attentively if you put on a record or tape and then start moving around the room, dusting furniture, straightening rugs, doing your income taxes, etc. Please don't allow your child to read or do homework while listening.

No Talking

Help your child learn good basic concert etiquette by refraining from speaking while the music is playing. Even if you are talking about the music, your conversation is a distraction. Let the music speak. Afterward, talk about it with your child.

HAVE A SPECIFIC LISTENING ASSIGNMENT

This is very important. Before the music begins, give your child something specific to listen for. Don't make it too complex; it can be something as simple as a certain instrument or group of instruments. Later, as your child becomes more musically sophisticated, make the listening assignment more complex. Here are some musical elements, along with a brief description of each, which you and your child can listen for and talk about.

Rhythm

Rhythm is the movement of music through time. Is the rhythm simple or complex? Is it a major element in the music? How does it change?

As your child learns more about reading and writing rhythm in Chapter 3, he will be better able to identify rhythms in music he hears.

Melody

Melody is a when groups of musical notes are played one after the other. Most music has a recognizable tune or melody. What role does the melody play? Does there seem to be more than one melody? How is the melody changed or altered during the music? Do sections of the melody repeat? How do they repeat?

Harmony

When two or more notes are sounded at the same time, we call that *harmony*. Can you tell when there is harmony (and when there is not)? How is harmony used to change the mood of the music?

Tone Color or Timbre

Tone color or *timbre* is the characteristic quality that distinguishes one voice or instrument from another. How many different instruments or voices can you hear? Which ones can you name? How does tone color affect the mood of the music?

Texture

Texture in music falls into one of the three categories. Most music employs combinations of these textures.

Monophonic music has no harmony and one single melody. A solo instrument or voice, with no other instruments or voices, would be *monophonic texture*.

Homophonic music has a main melody with accompaniment. An example is a church hymn. Most music we hear, including most popular music, is *homophonic texture*.

Polyphonic music has more than one melody at the same time. A "round" or "fugue" would have *polyphonic texture*.

Structure

Structure in music is based on repetition. Listen for repetition within the elements of Rhythm, Melody, Harmony, and Timbre. How does repetition help "hold" the music together?

LISTEN TO ONLY QUALITY RECORDINGS

Avoid scratchy records or tapes that hiss—sometimes a problem when you borrow recordings from the public library. The scratches and hisses are a distraction and take away from the quality of the music. This problem can be avoided if your public library has compact disks, since CDs are virtually noise-free. Also, try to have the best sound equipment you can afford. CD players are very affordable now and offer a whole new dimension to listening to music.

AFTERWARD—TALKING ABOUT IT

After you listen, discuss the music. Go over the listening assignment and ask your child about the elements he was supposed to listen for. Avoid subjective judgments at first. In other words, don't talk about whether or not your child found the music boring or exciting. Discuss the elements first, then talk about the effect the use of these elements had on the music.

By the way, it isn't necessary to sit down with a clipboard and go over all the elements of music one by one. Sometimes you can talk about one or two elements. Once your child becomes more familiar with them, you can ask him what he wants to talk about. The important thing is to *talk*—to discuss the music.

Once your child begins to listen *actively*—that is, once he begins to think about what he hears and compare it with other listening experiences—he will want to expand his listening activities.

WHEN AND WHERE TO LISTEN

A purposeful active listening program must have a time all its own. Set aside a certain time—it doesn't have to be every day, it can be once a week—and use that time to introduce your child to a variety of musical styles.

Active listening—listening for content—should not be done while studying or doing homework. There's nothing wrong with passive listening, but active listening is what we're after here. We want your child to listen to the music and then discuss it with you. For that reason you need to have a time and place that won't interfere with other activities.

You need a place without distractions where you and your child can be comfortable but alert. (Active listening doesn't lend itself well to napping.) Try to set aside a listening place as well as a listening time.

MUSICAL STYLES

This next section contains information on a variety of musical styles. In many instances, I've listed musical compositions that represent the style being discussed. Most are available in a variety of recorded formats. In some cases, notably music from non-western music traditions and popular music, there is simply too much material to choose from to come up with any type of representative "music" list. Instead, look under the specific ANSCR category. In the section on popular music I have listed some important performers and songwriters you may want to listen to, read about, and discuss with your child.

OPERA

An opera, like a play, usually tells a story. But it is more than a play with songs. (That's called a musical comedy and falls under the heading of popular music.) In an opera, the music continues throughout and enhances the mood and action of the story.

The story of an opera is called a *libretto*. Most operas are divided into acts, and each act tells a part of the story. The singers sing solos or in small groups or even with the entire cast singing at once. The most important songs in the opera are called *arias*. Sometimes, however, to fill in parts of the story, the characters must either speak or sing in a sort of monotone. These less-glamorous "speaking-songs" are called *recitative*.

Listening Suggestions—ANSCR Category B

Verdi, *Falstaff*

Rossini, *The Barber of Seville*
Humperdinck, *Hansel and Gretel*
Gershwin, *Porgy and Bess*

VOCAL AND CHORAL MUSIC

Vocal music is simply music that people sing, either with or without accompanying instruments. Vocal music is performed by one singer or a small group of singers, whereas choral music is sung by a choir or chorus of many singers, sometimes with solo singers.

In classical music, many solo singers give concerts of songs accompanied only by a pianist. Many of these classical songs are poems that are set to music.

Listening Suggestions—ANSCR Category D

Schubert, *Die Schone Mullerin* (The Fair Maid of the Mill)
Schumann, *Dichterliebe* (Poet's Love)
Brahms, *Four Serious Songs*
Wolf, *Morike Lieder*

Choral Music: Oratorios/Cantatas

Choral music often features a combination of a massive choir and an orchestra. Sometimes an organ is used instead of an orchestra. The music may also feature solo singers who take leading roles in the music. The music may be sacred or secular.

A grand choral work, such as an oratorio or a cantata, usually tells a story, often from the Bible. It is performed without action, costumes, or scenery, although solo singers often portray characters.

An oratorio generally demands a large choir or chorus or even two choirs, several soloists, and an orchestra. A cantata is a choral work on a smaller scale with only a few singers and instruments and sometimes without soloists.

Other kinds of choral music include symphonies in which a choir sings with the orchestra.

Listening Suggestions—ANSCR Category C

Handel, *Messiah* (Oratorio)
Orff, *Carmina Burana* (Cantata)
Brahms, *German Requiem*
Beethoven, *Symphony No. 9 in d minor*

BALLET AND DANCE

Music and movement go together like popcorn and movies. Dance cannot occur without music, and for some children, music cannot occur without dance.

Ballet is a form of dance that, like opera, tells a story. And like opera, ballet is normally performed on a stage with full scenery and costumes. The dancers tell the story with their movements, or they try to evoke a certain emotion to convey the mood of the music.

Other types of dancing include folk dancing and social dancing. These less formal dancing styles are designed as recreation—not for performance—although modern ballet and dance often use steps and movements made popular in social and folk dancing.

The best way to experience ballet is to see it, either live or on video tape. You may wish to listen to some ballet music with your child before watching. This will help to focus your child's attention on the music rather than the movement.

Listening Suggestions—ANSCR Category EB

Tchaikovsky, *The Nutcracker*
Delibes, *Coppelia*
Stravinsky, *Petrushka*
Copland, *Rodeo*

ORCHESTRAL MUSIC

Orchestral music requires a large group of players, normally a symphony orchestra with strings, brasses, woodwinds, and percussion. In the music of earlier composers such as Bach and Mozart, the orchestra contains a large string section but only small woodwind, brass, and percussion sections. Later composers wrote music for more instruments to get a wider range of sounds from the orchestra.

Listen to Benjamin Britten's *Young Person's Guide to the Orchestra* (or better yet, view it on video tape) before listening to other orchestral music.

Listening Suggestion—ANSCR Category E

Britten, *The Young Person's Guide to the Orchestra*

Variations

When a piece of classical music has the word "variations" in its title, it is made up of a theme or main melody and several *variations* on that melody. You can almost always hear the main melody in each variation. This type of music is easy to listen to and discuss.

Listening Suggestions—ANSCR Category EA

Brahms, *Variations on a Theme of Haydn*
Dohnanyi, *Variations on a Nursery Theme*
Rachmaninov, *Variations on a Theme of Paganini*
Ives, *Variations on America*

Suites

A suite is a group of short pieces, either played separately (one after the other) or as one continuous piece of music. The first suites were actually sets of dances.

Listening Suggestions—ANSCR Category EA

Handel, *Water Music*
Bizet, *L'Arlesienne Suites*
Stravinsky, *The Firebird*
Prokofiev, *Lieutenant Kije*

Descriptive Music

This kind of orchestral music aims to portray something in the music. The flow of notes should give the listener the impression of whatever the composer intends to depict, such as turbulent music for a battle or storm, fast rhythmic music for a race, quiet slow music for sadness, and so on. Descriptive music is fun for children to listen to, and the theme and variations are often easy to discuss.

Listening Suggestions—ANSCR Category EA

Rimsky-Korsakov, *Scheherezade*
Saint-Saens, *Carnival of the Animals*
Prokofiev, *Peter and the Wolf*
Dukas, *The Sorcerer's Apprentice*

Overtures

An overture is a short musical work designed to "open" a performance of an opera or a play. The music is supposed to put the audience in the right mood and often has bits and pieces of the music to come. In concerts, overtures are often played at the beginning as an opener or "show piece" for the orchestra.

Listening Suggestions—ANSCR Category EA

Beethoven, *Egmont Overture*
Rossini, *William Tell Overture*
Berlioz, *Roman Carnival Overture*
Brahms, *Academic Festival Overture*

Concertos

A concerto is a long piece of music to be played by a solo performer with a symphony orchestra. The soloist is the star, and the music was and is often written with a specific performer in mind, to show off the performer's talent or abilities. A concerto can also be thought of as a sort of "duel" between the orchestra and the soloist. (Sometimes it sounds more like a brawl.)

Listening Suggestions—ANSCR Category EC

Bach, *Brandenberg Concertos*
Mozart, *Piano Concert No. 21 in C Major*
Tchaikovsky, *Violin Concerto in D Major*
Rodrigo, *Concierto de Aranjuez* (for guitar)

Symphonies

The symphony is the best known of the classical styles of music. A symphony is a major work. Composers spend (and spent) a lot of time writing a single symphony. A symphony has separate sections called movements—normally three or four movements to a symphony. Though each movement is made up of contrasting musical ideas containing different themes, all the movements are woven together to form a unified work. When listening to a symphony with your child, pay particular attention to recurring melodies in the different movements.

Listening Suggestions—ANSCR Category ES

Mozart, *Symphony No. 40 in g minor*
Beethoven, *Symphony No. 5 in c minor*
Prokofiev, *Symphony No. 1 in D Major*
Shostakovich, *Symphony No. 5 in d minor*

CHAMBER MUSIC

Chamber music is a type of classical music that is played by small groups of two to five musicians. Each musician in a chamber group has a different part, and everyone's part is important.

Listening Suggestions—ANSCR Category F

Bartok, *String Quartet No. 2 in a minor*
Brahms, *Horn Trio in E♭ Major*
Haydn, *String Quartet No. 38 in E♭ Major*
Stravinsky, *L'Histoire Du Soldat*

MUSIC FOR ONE INSTRUMENT

Classical music contains a wealth of music that can be played on one instrument. Most of this music is for keyboard instruments, particularly the piano. This is because the keyboard allows all the fingers and thumbs of both hands to produce notes. Furthermore, the notes played can range greatly in pitch, and the volume or tone of each note can be controlled by the performer.

Other solo classical instruments include the guitar, violin, and cello. These instruments can sound more than one string at a time and play a wide variety of sounds as does the keyboard.

Listening Suggestions—ANSCR Category G

Mussorgsky, *Pictures at an Exhibition* (piano)
Bach, *Cello Suites 1-6* (cello)
Paganini, *Caprices 1-24* (violin)
Debussy, *Syrinx* (flute)

BAND MUSIC

When most people think of a band, they envision a marching band parading down the street or performing for halftime at a football game. Actually, marching bands represent only one type of band. There are also concert or symphonic bands—the wind and percussion equivalent of the symphony orchestra—military bands, brass bands, jazz (dance) bands, Dixieland bands, and more. The list goes on and on.

Look in the ANSCR Band classification (H) for marching and concert band materials. Check under the Popular Music category (M) for jazz, Dixieland, and so forth. Under listening suggestions I have listed some notable composers who have written music for concert band. In addition, a wealth of orchestra material has been arranged for band and is available on tapes and records.

Listening Suggestions—ANSCR Category H

Music by: Henry Fillmore, Edwin Franko Goldman, Morton Gould, Percy Grainger, Clare Grundman, Howard Hanson, Paul Hindemuth, Gustav Holst, Karl King, W. Francis McBeth, Alfred Reed, and John Philip Sousa.

POPULAR MUSIC

Popular music is the music a child hears on radio and sees on

MTV. Style in popular music is reflected more in the personality of the performer than in just about any other kind of music. Popular music styles include jazz, rock, soul, rhythm and blues, country-western, and a whole new style of Christian popular music that grew out of gospel and rock.

For listening examples, look under the specific "M" classification for the music you are interested in; i.e., MA for Pop, MC for Country, MJ for Jazz, etc.

Musicals

Broadway musicals and movie musicals have given us scores of memorable tunes. Below are some of my favorites.

Listening Suggestions—ANSCR Category K

Arlen, *The Wizard of Oz*
Beatles, *Yellow Submarine*
Berlin, *Annie Get Your Gun*
Bernstein/Sondheim, *West Side Story*
Brown, *Singin' in the Rain*
Jacobs/Casey, *Grease*
Rodgers/Hammerstein, *The Sound of Music*

Soul

Soul music is Black music grounded in the African-American experience.

Listening Suggestions

Performers/songwriters: James Brown, Ray Charles, Sam Cooke, Aretha Franklin, Wilson Pickett, Otis Redding, Tina Turner.

Pop

Pop music surrounds most of us, whether we like it or not. Try to escape it for a week. It's not possible.

Listening Suggestions—ANSCR Category MA

Performers/groups: Michael Jackson, Elton John, Barry Manilow, Diana Ross, Bruce Springsteen, Beach Boys, Chicago.

Country-Western

Country-western music tells stories of "real" blue-collar life: jobs and money and bad love affairs.

Listening Suggestions—ANSCR Category MC

Performers/songwriters: Roy Acuff, Johnny Cash, Tennessee Ernie Ford, Emmylou Harris, Brenda Lee, Dolly Parton, Patsy Cline, Charley Pride, Kenny Rogers, Hank Williams, Senior.

Jazz

Jazz isn't necessarily screeching or "weird"; a lot of it is beautiful and almost as easy to follow as any other kind of music.

Listening Suggestions—ANSCR Category MJ

Performers/composers: Louis Armstrong, Joe "King" Oliver, Earl Hines, Harry James, Count Basie, Fats Waller, Tommy Dorsey, Benny Goodman, Glen Miller, Woody Herman, Buddy Rich, Miles Davis, Dizzy Gillespie, Clark Terry, Charlie Parker, Dave Brubeck, Oscar Peterson, John Coltrane, Art Blakley.

Blues

Blues singers are usually Black and sing about bad times. This is the music of the rural and urban poor.

Listening Suggestions—ANSCR Category MR

Performers/songwriters: Blind Lemon Jefferson, B.B. King, Huddie Ledbetter, Bessie Smith, T. Bone Walker, Muddy Waters.

Rock Music

Try classic rock music of the late 1950s through the 1960s.

Listening Suggestions—ANSCR Category MR

Performers/groups: Bill Haley and the Comets, Little Richard, Chuck Berry, Carl Perkins, Elvis Presley, Jerry Lee Lewis, Beatles, Jimi Hendrix, The Rolling Stones.

Folk Music

Folk or protest music began in the 1930s and became most popular in the 1960s and 1970s.

Listening Suggestions—ANSCR Category P

Performers/songwriters: Joan Baez; Crosby, Stills, Nash, and Young; Bob Dylan; Carole King; Simon and Garfunkel.

NATIONAL AND INTERNATIONAL FOLK AND ETHNIC MUSIC

Music is something that people everywhere need to enhance their lives. Music has tremendous power to affect human feelings, especially when used to accompany words and movement in singing and dancing. Throughout the world, people have developed many distinctive ways of making music.

Listening Suggestions—ANSCR Category Q

The variety of folk and ethnic music makes it impossible to suggest specific pieces. Look under ANSCR Category P or Q by country or ethnic group. If your family background is Russian, for example, you may like Russian folk music.

INDIAN MUSIC

Traditional Indian music is performed by small groups of musicians. A singer (or principal player) leads the music, often on a stringed instrument called a *sitar*. The sitar player is supported by a few accompanying musicians—often just a drummer and one other musician.

Indian music is mostly improvised (made up as the musicians go along). The purpose of Indian music is to create and sustain a particular emotion or mood, such as joy, sorrow, or peace. To do this, the performers choose a particular scale of notes for their piece. The scale and notes are called a *raga*.

CHINESE MUSIC

Unlike Indian music, Chinese traditional music is composed, not improvised. It may be written down or handed down from teacher to pupil and memorized, but it does not change from one performance to another.

Chinese music aims to describe things, particularly scenes and situations, and so has to be very precise in its effect on listeners. A wide range of instruments may be played together; a Chinese orchestra makes a great variety of sounds.

One of the principal forms of Chinese music is opera. Productions are highly stylized: some actors paint their faces in different colors to represent their roles.

JAPANESE MUSIC

The music of Japan resembles that of China in several ways: Japanese music consists mainly of composed melody that is either written or handed down. It is often descriptive; music is used in stylized theater productions, like the opera in China.

Japanese music sounds different from Chinese music, mainly because it uses different scales to build its melodies. With enough practice listening, your child will be able to tell the difference between Chinese and Japanese music.

INDONESIAN MUSIC

Music of the Indonesian islands is very unusual because of both its instruments and its scale systems. As in China and Japan, the music is principally a composed melody that is written or handed down. One unusual aspect of Indonesian music has to do with the large orchestras, called *gamelans*, that play the music. A gamelan may have anywhere from thirty to forty players.

Most orchestras in the world consist of musicians who play one of several available standard instruments. A gamelan is totally different. Each town or village may have its own gamelan, and the instruments of the gamelan are made by one instrument maker in that town. They are tuned to the notes of the Indonesian scales, but the pitch of the notes is not standard. Each instrument maker produces slightly different instruments, so one gamelan sounds different from another.

AUSTRALIAN MUSIC

Aborigines—the original Black inhabitants of Australia—have developed some of the most unusual traditional music in the world. Cut off from the rest of the world until Europeans began to settle Australia two centuries ago, Aborigines developed their music in total isolation for several thousand years.

Aborigines make music to accompany rituals and dances. The rhythmic style, which can be very complex, is handed down and not written. The music is vocal, with singers and chanters producing all kinds of vocal sounds as well as words. Aboriginal music does not adhere to any particular system of notation, and Aborigines never developed instruments that play the notes of any known scale. The vocal music is accompanied by the beating of simple percussion instruments, such as sticks and rattles, and hand-clapping. In addition, there may be the unusual sound of the Aborigine's single main musical instrument—the *didgeridoo*.

AFRICAN MUSIC

Musically, Africa consists of two distinct nations. In North Africa, the music belongs to the Asian melodic tradition and basically consists of a fluid musical line. This is because North Africa is mainly Arab and is thus linked to the Middle East. South of the Sahara, however, a completely different kind of music is to be heard—the music of black Africa.

Music plays a central role in the lives of tribal Africans, perhaps more so than in any other part of the world. This does not mean that all Africans are professional musicians, but most tribal Africans are musical and spend a great deal of time (compared to Americans, for example) singing and dancing.

African music has one special feature: its use of rhythm, which is more highly developed than in any other traditional music in the world, with the possible exception of music of the Aborigines.

EUROPEAN MUSIC

Music we call "classical" music came from Europe and Russia, but these countries have a long tradition of music made by ordinary people for their own pleasure. This music consists of folk songs and dances, the tunes of which, usually composed long ago, are handed down from generation to generation.

AMERICAN MUSIC

The continents of North and South America have a fascinating range of music. This is because of the vast area and the fact that they are home to many different peoples whose ancestors came from other parts of the world. Many of their original styles of music are preserved, but new and exciting kinds of music have come about and developed as diverse peoples mixed.

American Indian Music

The first inhabitants of America were the American Indians, who crossed from Asia many thousands of years ago. In North America, their music has changed little. Their songs and dances help the Indian tribes to preserve their identity. The music features simple melodies, often repeated many times to any words the singer cares to sing. American Indian instruments include flutes, whistles, rattles, and drums.

Latin America

In Latin America (Central and South America), there is little left of the original Indian tradition. Most of the folk songs and dances have tunes of Spanish origin. The way in which pairs of singers or instruments often perform a melody, with one always singing a third (three notes) below the tune, is a characteristic feature of Spanish music. However, the music may also use Indian panpipes or other instruments made of wood or pottery.

Caribbean Music

The African heritage is particularly strong in Jamaica, Trinidad, and Haiti. The songs and dances of the Caribbean contain many of the call-and-response patterns of African music.

Jamaica and Trinidad have produced two famous song styles: reggae and calypso. They feature a strong but relaxed beat and place great importance on words.

Trinidad gave the world a completely new musical sound in the 1940s with the invention of the steel drum. Steel drums (called pans) were originally made from oil drums, and have panels of metal that produce notes with a ringing sound when beaten with mallets.

North America

The ethnic and folk traditions of North America reflect the variety of people who have populated that part of the world. Here the music of Black people transported from Africa to work as slaves combined with the melody and harmony of European tradition to create gospel, jazz, rock, soul, and country music, styles that are described elsewhere.

LIVE PERFORMANCES

In addition to setting up a program of listening to recorded music, you and your child can and should attend live performances. Many opportunities probably exist in your community to hear fine music "live." Go!

Community Performances

Your community may have a community band or orchestra, which probably plays for local events or in the summer in a local park. Check with the local Chamber of Commerce or City Hall.

Professional Performances

These can include a professional symphony orchestra, professional concert band, or visiting national performers. If there is a military base near you, check about bands playing on base. Most large installations have a band that usually performs many times during the year and throughout the community. Best of all, most of these performances are free.

Church Performances

In many churches, choirs perform a cantata or other major musical work at least once during the year. Some larger church choirs perform evening concerts on a regular basis. These performances may or may not be part of a religious service. Sometimes there is a charge, but more often a "free-will" offering is taken.

College Performances

Call the nearest college or university music department and ask to be put on their mailing list. They will be only too happy to oblige. You will receive notice of many fine musical events you and your child can attend together, often for very little money or none at all.

School Performances

Call or visit your local high school. Ask when their music programs are. You can do the same for junior high school. Your child may have friends in these groups. Who knows, perhaps attending one or two concerts may inspire your child to join the choir, band, or orchestra.

TELEVISION AND RADIO

The wise and careful viewer can find many programs of musical quality on television and on radio, especially on public TV and radio. Check your weekly local newspaper listings and call or write your local public television or radio station and ask for a program guide. (Caution: When you do this, you might be asked to support public television and public radio. That's OK. You *should*.)

7.

CAREERS IN MUSIC

In the little town where I grew up, the only "music professionals" I ever came in contact with were the high school band director and choir director. And since the band director was the choir director, I'm talking about one person! It wasn't until I went to college that I became aware of the many other opportunities, besides teaching, that exist for those who choose to make music a career.

This chapter provides a selected overview of some of the many careers in music-related fields. You and your child can use this information as a springboard for discussions about the differences between music as a "vocation" and music as an "avocation."

MUSIC TEACHER

For most children, their first encounter with a professional musician is with the school music teacher.

There are music teachers in both public and private schools, and most of them have, at minimum, a four-year college degree in music education. In addition, school music teachers, like all teachers, must hold a teaching certificate in the state in which they teach. Music teachers in schools often specialize in band, orchestra, choir, or general music.

High school music programs often include courses in general

music, fine arts appreciation, music theory, or music history. These classes are also taught by music specialists.

In some larger school systems, especially where there is a high school for the performing arts, there may even be teachers who specialize in musical theater or who only teach specific instruments or voice.

Positions exist for supervisors or coordinators of music in some larger school districts. These are often administrative positions involving the supervision of other music teachers, maintaining and developing music budgets, and so forth.

Public and private school music teachers also often serve in their communities as conductors of church choirs, community bands and orchestras, and music-related city recreational programs.

College music teachers teach school music teachers and specialize in one or two areas such as music theory, music history, music education, musicology, performance, electronic music, composition, conducting, or music therapy. In many cases, college teachers come from the ranks of successful professional musicians or public or private school music teachers. A college music educator, however, usually must have earned at least a master's degree in music. Sometimes a doctorate is required.

Private teachers may be school or college music teachers or professional musicians who teach as a second source of income, or they may teach privately full time. Private teachers teach a specific instrument or voice, one on one, to students for a fee.

MUSIC THERAPY

Music therapists work with physically and mentally handicapped people in hospitals, special education facilities, clinics, mental health centers, nursing homes, and prisons. Some have their own private practices.

To become a music therapist requires a four-year college degree as well as several months of internship in one of the facilities mentioned above. Music therapists combine training in music, teaching, and therapy to help persons with disabilities improve their physical and mental health. As I said before, everybody loves music. *Everybody*.

PERFORMANCE

It is easy for young people to get caught up in the glamour of wanting to become a professional performer, but the truth is, opportunities are very limited and the competition is stiff. To make it as a performing musician takes more than talent. It also takes a lot of stamina and a certain amount of luck. People make it, and the rewards for those lucky few are tremendous.

Most performing musicians have to rely on income from other jobs to pay the bills between performances. Many professional performers also teach privately.

Listed below are some positions performing musicians fill. In many cases, these positions do not pay enough for the performer to make a living without teaching privately or having another job.

Vocal

Armed Forces Bands/Orchestras
Broadway/Professional Theater
Church Choir/Soloist
Concert Choral Group/Soloist
Jazz Band/Nightclub
Opera Chorus/Soloist
Radio, TV Shows/Commercials
Rock Group Singer
Symphony Chorus

Instrumental

Armed Forces Bands/Orchestra
Broadway/Professional Theater Orchestra
Clinician
Concert Soloist
Jazz Band/Nightclub
Professional Concert Band
Radio, TV Shows/Commercials
Rock Group Musician
Small Ensemble
Symphony Orchestra

CHURCH MUSIC

Most church and temple musicians are employed part-time, although large congregations may have a full-time music director or minister of music. Church or temple musicians are often required to compose or arrange music for services and must be familiar with the theology and liturgy of worship for their denomination.

Some of the positions held by church or temple musicians include:

Organist
Choir Director
Minister of Music
Liturgist
Choir Member/Soloist

COMPOSER

Composers write music for school performing groups, radio and television commercials, movies and TV shows, recording artists, and professional symphony orchestras, to name a few.

When a composer is hired to write music for a specific performing group or for a special occasion, that is called a "commission." Composers, like writers, are usually paid "by the piece," not by the hour. In other words, they write a composition and then try to get someone to buy it.

When a composer's composition is published, recorded, or used in radio, television, or movies, the composer is paid a royalty. Royalties can become a composer's most important source of income—if he writes and sells a lot of music.

CONDUCTOR

Conductors, like many professional musicians, often rely on supplemental income from teaching or guest appearances. Some symphony conductors with international reputations can become wealthy, but most make a very modest income. Just about all of the musical groups listed so far require a conductor (or music director).

MUSIC INDUSTRY

The music industry includes retail, wholesale, manufacturing, importing, exporting, publishing, recording, repair and rebuilding, tuning, and other businesses in which music plays a significant role. A career in the music industry requires training and education in both music and business. One of the fastest-growing segments of the music industry deals with computers and music-related computer equipment and software.

Within the broad spectrum of the music industry there are literally hundreds of positions. These include:

Music Publisher or Editor
Writing, Manufacturing, and Distribution of Music Software
Importer or Wholesaler of Instruments and Accessories
Manager/Booking Agent
Retail Music Dealer
Tuner/Piano Technician
Instrument Repair

TELEVISION/RADIO

The television and radio industries encompass a wide range of careers, including some that have already been mentioned, such as composer, performer, conductor, etc. Musicians also work in the broadcast media clearing copyrights and licensing music for on-air performance.

Television and radio stations, production houses, and post-production facilities hire music-trained individuals to help with production, host shows (disc jockey/video jockey), and act as program directors, determining the format or type of music used on the air.

A career in the broadcast industry could include positions such as:

Copyright Clearance Administrator
Music License Administrator
Music Editor
Sound Mixer
Post Production/Scoring

Disc Jockey/Video Jockey
Program Director
Music Adviser/Researcher

MUSIC LIBRARIAN

A music librarian is a specialist who has training in the library sciences and in music. Colleges and public libraries both offer opportunities for people with this kind of background and skill, as do professional music performance groups and even some radio and TV stations.

Music librarians conduct research, catalog music-related materials, maintain music files, and select music materials for purchase. Some opportunities for music librarians exist in radio, television, and motion pictures.

Institutions and organizations that employ music librarians include:

College/University Music Departments
Large Public Libraries
Professional Orchestras/Bands/Choruses
Radio/TV Stations

OTHER CAREERS IN MUSIC

In addition to the careers in music mentioned above, opportunities exist in the field of musicology (the science of music), music law, architecture and acoustics, and arts administration. Most large newspapers and many magazines hire a music reporter to cover or review music events and concerts.

As this brief overview shows, a career in music can involve much more than learning to sing or to play an instrument. Thousands of people are employed in music-related professions all over the world.

For more information about careers in music, write to any of the associations or unions listed below. Shelly Field's book, *Career Opportunities in the Music Industry* offers a comprehensive guide to music as a vocation and *The Young Performer's Guide*, by Brian

Padol and Alan Simon, offers advice to young people seeking a career in show business.

CAREER-RELATED ASSOCIATIONS AND UNIONS

AMERICAN ASSOCIATION FOR MUSIC THERAPY
P.O. Box 27177
Philadelphia, PA 19118

National nonprofit membership organization serving the music therapy profession.

AMERICAN FEDERATION OF MUSICIANS
Suite 600, Paramount Building
1501 Broadway
New York, NY 10036

Bargaining representative of professional musicians in all phases of the music industry.

AMERICAN GUILD OF ORGANISTS
815 Second Avenue, Suite 318
New York, NY 10017

National association for the promotion of organ playing.

AMERICAN MUSIC CONFERENCE
303 East Wacker Drive, Suite 1214
Chicago, IL 60601

Promotes the benefits of participating in music to the American public.

AMERICAN MUSICOLOGICAL SOCIETY, INC.
201 South 34th Street
University of Pennsylvania
Philadelphia, PA 19104

Dedicated to the study of the science of music.

AMERICAN SOCIETY OF COMPOSERS, AUTHORS, AND PUBLISHERS (ASCAP)
1 Lincoln Plaza
New York, NY 10023

A nonprofit membership organization that licenses, on a non-exclusive basis, the non-dramatic right of public performance of its members' musical compositions.

AMERICAN SYMPHONY ORCHESTRA LEAGUE
777 14th Street, N.W., Suite 500
Washington, DC 20005

National service organization for orchestras; serves the coordinating, research, and educational needs of symphony orchestras.

BROADCAST MUSIC, INC. (BMI)
320 W. 57th Street
New York, NY 10019

Acquires performing rights from songwriters, composers, and publishers and in turn grants licenses for the public performance of the music.

MUSIC CRITICS ASSOCIATION, INC.
7 Pine Court
Westfield, NJ 07090

Acts as an educational medium for the promotion of high standards of music criticism in the American press.

MUSIC EDUCATOR'S NATIONAL CONFERENCE (MENC)
1902 Association Drive
Reston, VA 22091

Has the advancement of music education as its principal objective.

MUSIC TEACHERS NATIONAL ASSOCIATION
617 Vine Street, Suite 1432
Cincinnati, OH 45202

Serves the studio music teacher in America at all levels of instruction.

NATIONAL ASSOCIATION OF PROFESSIONAL BAND INSTRUMENT REPAIR TECHNICIANS (NAPBIRT)
P.O. Box 51
Normal, IL 61761

Provides a central agency for the exchange of information and implements a code of ethics that exemplifies the dignity and credibility of the profession.

NATIONAL ASSOCIATION OF SCHOOLS OF MUSIC
11250 Roger Bacon Drive, Suite 21
Reston, VA 22090

The accrediting agency for educational programs in music.

NATIONAL FEDERATION OF MUSIC CLUBS
1336 North Delaware
Indianapolis, IN 46202

Seeks to bring together music clubs, organizations, and individuals directly associated with music.

NATIONAL MUSIC PUBLISHERS' ASSOCIATION, INC.
205 East 42nd Street
New York, NY 10017

Association of music publishers in the United States.

8.

TEACHING MATERIALS

A variety of materials exists to help you teach your child about music. In this chapter I will discuss some of them and tell you where to find them. Prices are the approximate retail prices, which were obtained from catalogs and stores. Please remember that prices change, so check with the retailer or catalog before buying or ordering.

TEACHING AIDS

Many teaching aids can be purchased or ordered through your local music store or educator's supply outlet. (Most communities have a store where teachers go to get bulletin board materials, etc.) Some items, such as dry-wipe markers, are also available at office supply stores.

Staff Paper

Staff paper comes in a variety of styles, sizes, and prices, ranging from single sheets, to tablets, to wideline paper, to large pads. Buy the least expensive you can find. There is no need to get "professional" quality staff paper. Pad of 50 sheets, $3.00.

Laminated Staff Paper

Laminated staff paper can be used over and over with a dry-wipe marker to practice writing notes and music symbols. You can even make your own laminated staff paper if you have access to a laminator. $5.00 per sheet.

Laminated Keyboard

If you don't have a piano, a laminated keyboard can help your child begin to learn the relationship between "written" notes and keys on the piano. It can be used with dry-wipe markers. $3.50.

Musical Flashcards

Musical flashcards are useful for drill in teaching musical terms, notes, signs, key signatures, etc. If you have a computer, there are even computerized musical flashcard programs. $3.75.

Activity Books and Workbooks

Music activity books include puzzles and exercises that reinforce learning note names, musical terms, music history, composers' names, etc. Activity books and workbooks aren't expensive and provide an entertaining way to get your child to drill on fundamentals of music. $3.00 to $6.00.

GAMES

Children love to play games and the ones listed below are only a few of the many available from music stores, mail order dealers, and educational supply houses.

Music Bingo

The well-known principles of bingo serve as the starting point in a family game that provides an exciting and educational way for children to learn the fundamentals of music. $8.00.

Dominotes

Based on the age-old game of dominoes, this game has notes and rests instead of spots. Children quickly learn about note and rest values in order to accumulate points. $20.

Music Maestro II

This board game about musical instruments, past and present, features a cassette tape and is actually five games in one. Games teach the sounds, shapes and functions of forty-eight instruments played in classical, bluegrass, jazz, and rock ensembles. $25.

Mozart Melody Dicer

This ingenious game allows players to compose music by throwing dice. At the end of the game, the player has a completed piece of music, which can be played on a piano or keyboard. The Mozart Melody Dicer is based on the composing practices of Mozart. There is also a Scott Joplin Melody Dicer that features the sounds of ragtime music. $16.

Forward March

Players take turns answering questions on notes, intervals, scales, chords, key signatures, rhythm, and music vocabulary in this board game. The game is unique in that it has three levels of difficulty, and players on different levels can play together, which makes it a perfect family game. $30.

Oldies But Goodies Board Game

This trivia board game features two cassette tapes and over 3,500 rock n' roll questions from the '50's, '60's, and '70's. $25.

Play the Beats

This board game helps children learn notes and rests, measure counting, and music symbols. Players move along a continuous music staff, marked off in measures with time signatures. First player to reach "Fine" wins. $12.

COMPUTER SOFTWARE

Music-related computer software is available for virtually every brand of computer. Many entertaining programs exist to provide the drill necessary for your child to learn the fundamentals of music.

The programs listed below represent only a portion of all the music education software available. Since new titles are being introduced every day, you would be well-advised to ask about updates or new versions of any program that interests you.

Software can be obtained from computer stores, from music dealers, and from catalogs. Computer stores, as a rule, don't stock much music instruction software, but they can order just about any title you want as long as you supply the name of the publisher. Music dealers who handle computer software probably have more music-related titles on hand, are better able to answer your questions, and may advise you about software that will best meet your child's needs.

One of the country's largest music dealers specializing in computer software is Sam Ash Educational Services, listed in the resources section at the end of this chapter.

Before you buy a program, ask about reviewing it either at home or in the store. Policies differ from store to store, but, if possible, try before you buy.

Alfred's Basic Piano Theory Software

This software covers the musical and theoretical concepts taught in Alfred's Basic Piano Library. Each level contains a carefully arranged sequence of games that present and review material in an entertaining manner. Topics include note names, rhythms, musical terminology, scales, chords, and intervals. The programs are intended for students age seven and up. All instructions appear on the computer screen. MIDI keyboard optional. For Apple II, Commodore 64, IBM, Atari ST 3.5, Yamaha C1, and Macintosh. Retail: $50 to $60. Alfred Publishing, 16380 Roscoe Blvd., Box 10003, Van Nuys, CA 91410.

Early Music Skills

This program is designed to drill beginning students on lines and spaces of the musical staff and aural and visual recognition of notes moving up or down by step or skip. For Apple, Commodore, IBM, and Yamaha. Retail: $40. Electronic Courseware Systems, 1210 Lancaster Drive, Champaign, IL 61821.

Keyboard Tutor

This teaches elementary students the names of the keys on the keyboard and matches the keys to notes on the staff; drills reinforce these concepts. MIDI and non-MIDI. For Apple, IBM, and Yamaha. Retail: $40. Electronic Courseware Systems, 1210 Lancaster Drive, Champaign, IL 61821.

Musical Stairs

Musical Stairs is an aural-visual drill and practice game on intervals, for students from kindergarten through eighth grade. It uses the keyboard to drill randomly selected white-key intervals within the range of one octave. After numbering the white keys one to eight and relating them to the staff, the program displays and plays intervals; a student determines the size of the interval and enters his response on the on-screen keyboard. MIDI and non-MIDI. For Apple, Commodore, IBM, Atari, and Yamaha. Retail: $40. Electronic Courseware Systems, 1210 Lancaster Drive, Champaign, IL 61821.

Music Flash Cards

This program consists of three diskettes with nine lessons each, intended for students of the elementary through junior high grades. Disk One covers note names and rhythmic values; Disk Two includes lessons on major, minor, and modal scales and key signatures; Disk Three covers intervals and basic chords. In all these lessons the computer keeps score and displays an evaluation of the student's work at the end of each lesson. Non-MIDI. For Apple and Commodore. Retail: $40 per disk, $100 for the set. Electronic Courseware Systems, 1210 Lancaster Drive, Champaign, IL 61821.

Note Speller

Note Speller drills identification of note names in the treble, bass, and alto clefs. As notes are displayed on the staff, the student types the note names as quickly as possible to spell words from four to seven letters in length; the faster the student responds, the higher the score. Note Speller is intended for students from kindergarten through eighth grade; users can choose from four levels of difficulty for each drill. Non-MIDI. For Apple, Commodore, IBM, and Yamaha. Retail: $40. Electronic Courseware Systems, 1210 Lancaster Drive, Champaign, IL 61821.

Music Studio

Music Studio requires an Apple IIgs with 512 RAM and a mouse or an IBM-compatible computer. A blank formatted disk allows students to save their creations, and a printer is necessary to print out songs.

Users can alter pre-programmed songs, or they may compose original songs. Once a piece is composed or altered, the student may either hear it played back or print it out.

One of the unique features of the program is the Music Paintbox, which allows students to "paint" music onto the screen using several sizes of colored rectangles instead of traditional music notation. They can listen to the composition while watching it on the screen or actually see it momentarily disappear from the screen note by note as it is performed. For Apple IIgs and IBM. Retail: $70. Activision, 3885 Bohannon Drive, Menlo Park, CA 94025.

Music Construction Kit

Music Construction Kit requires an Apple IIgs with 256 RAM, a mouse, and a printer for hard copy output. It is also advertised as a music composition program. It includes pull-down menus, mouse-oriented music editing, and two timbres (voices) at a time. Music Construction Kit has useful editing options such as cut and paste and block copying and printing. For Apple IIgs, IBM, and Commodore. Retail: $20. Electronic Arts, 1820 Gateway Drive, San Mateo, CA 94404.

The Miracle Piano Teaching System for Nintendo®

Imagine this: A video game that doesn't feature exploding vegetables! OK, so it *does* involve flying "duck-notes" the player can pelt with tomatoes by correctly naming notes on the staff. At least you don't have to watch that little guy with the moustache get a concussion by beating his head against a floating brick wall!

The Miracle Piano Teaching System by the Software Tool

works helps teach children (and fun-loving adults) how to begin to master playing the keyboard.

The system features a MIDI-compatible keyboard with forty-nine full-size, velocity-sensitive keys. The keyboard, which has 128 digital instrument sounds and effects built in, plugs into any IBM-PC or compatible, Amiga Computer, or Nintendo® or Super Nintendo® Entertainment System. Through a series of customized lessons, it teaches a variety of techniques, including finding keys on the piano, naming notes, learning rhythm, and so on.

According to Software Toolworks, "the average student with no prior musical knowledge should be able to complete the course in six to 12 months. By then, the child should be able to read music notation, play with two hands using common chords and rhythms, learn new pieces of music on your own, and perform with other musicians."

The Miracle Piano Teaching System cannot replace a "live" piano teacher. It can't provide meaningful feedback or "human" encouragement. For example: It doesn't teach the proper way to curve the hand when playing piano.

What the System can do is take some of the drudgery out of practice. The games and lessons are fun, and many kids seem willing to spend as much time with the Miracle System as they do with other video games.

Depending on the system you are hooking up to, the Miracle Piano Teaching System sells for anywhere from $300 to about $400, which isn't cheap, but considering what you get, it might be worth it. For IBM, Amiga, Nintendo®, Super Nintendo®. The Software Toolworks, 60 Leveroni Court, Novato, CA 94949.

SOURCES

If you have trouble locating music-teaching materials locally, the companies listed below handle many of the products mentioned in this book. Most will send you a catalog if you write.

ABA MUSIC FOR CHILDREN
217 Madrona SE
Salem, OR 97302

Specializing in K-6 classroom music with emphasis on Orff-Schulwerk.

ACCURA MUSIC/ABILITY DEVELOPMENT
79 East State Street
P.O. Box 4260
Athens, OH 45701

Recordings, music, and books for the Suzuki Method.

EDUCATIONAL ACTIVITIES
1937 Grand Avenue
Baldwin, NY 11510

Producer and distributor of Hap Palmer, Ella Jenkins, Rosemary Hallum, Buzz Glass, Cathy Slonecki — children's sing-along LPs, cassettes, and videos.

FRIENDSHIP HOUSE
29313 Clemens Road #2-G
P.O. Box 450978
Cleveland, OH 44145-0623

Musical gifts, games, and teaching supplies.

GAMBLE MUSIC COMPANY
312 South Wabash
Chicago, IL 60604

A variety of musical merchandise.

GENERAL MUSIC STORE
19880 State Line Road
South Bend, IN 46637

Musical gifts, games, and teaching supplies.

LMI OF ITASCA, ILLINOIS
127 N. Walnut Street
Itasca, IL 60143

K-8 music products for education.

MEL BAY PUBLICATIONS, INC.
#4 Industrial Drive
Pacific, MO 63069

Specializing in books for guitar and other fretted instruments.

MUSIC IN MOTION
109 Spanish Village, Suite 645
Dallas, TX 75248

Music education and gifts.

SAM ASH EDUCATIONAL SERVICES
270 Duffy Avenue
Hicksville, NY 11801

Traditional instruments as well as computers and software.

MUSIC MINUS ONE, INC.
50 South Buckhout Street
Irvington, NY 10533

Sing-along tapes and CDs; play-along records and tapes.

THE MUSIC STAND
1 Rockdale Plaza
Lebanon, NH 03766

Gifts and ideas for the performing arts.

Coda

AND ANOTHER THING ...

If you got here by going through the book from the beginning, you already know what a Coda is. If you didn't, you'll just have to guess.

And now, time for ...

TRUE CONFESSIONS

This book doesn't contain everything there is to know on the subject of music. I hope you're not surprised. After all, music has been around since the first caveman took a hollow log and used it to beat on the second caveman—thereby inventing what we know today as "rap" music. Any activity that has been around that long would take up far more pages than you could fit into one book.

Among the musical elements left out of this book were thirty-second notes, alto and tenor clefs, and about seventy billion Italian music terms that all mean "Play faster, Luigi, the pasta's about to boil over!" I left out some other stuff too, but at the moment I can't think what it is.

If you want to know more—and I sincerely hope you do—there are books in the 780 Dewey Decimal Classification (Music) in your local public library that can take you and your child as far into the fascinating world of music as you want to go. Besides, learning about music should be a lifelong pursuit. I hope you and your child pursue it for at least that long.

BIG FINISH

Actually, it's not a big finish at all. I just want to say I hope you and your child have enjoyed learning about music together. I hope it gives you yet another special subject to talk about, along with homework, boyfriends or girlfriends, clothes, clouds, sports, television, movies, politics, teachers, cars, religion, Chinese food, toys, life, and knock-knock jokes. (Your actual list of conversation topics may vary. Parental discretion is advised. Especially when it comes to those stupid knock-knock jokes!) Now, if you'll excuse me, I gotta go look up the phone number for "Bat Busters."

Thanks for listening. And good luck!

APPENDICES

A. Glossary of Music Terms

B. Music-Related Organizations

APPENDIX A
GLOSSARY OF MUSIC TERMS

A CAPELLA—(It.) Unaccompanied singing.

A TEMPO—(It.) Resume earlier tempo.

ACCELERANDO—(It.) Becoming quicker.

ACCENT—Make stronger. Emphasize.

ACCIDENTAL—A sharp, flat, or natural not found in the key signature.

ACCOMPANIMENT—Any part or parts that back up the principal parts.

AD LIBITUM—(Lat.) At the performer's discretion.

ADAGIETTO—(It.) Somewhat faster than *adagio*.

ADAGIO—(It.) Slow.

AGITATO—(It.) Agitated.

AL CODA—(It.) Go to the Coda.

AL FINE—(It.) To the end. Usually with *da capo* or *dal segno*.

ALLA BREVE—(It.) Double the tempo (with half note as the beat). Cut time.

ALLARGANDO—(It.) Getting slower.

ALLEGRETTO—(It.) Not as fast as *allegro*.

ALLEGRO—(It.) Fast.

ANDANTE—(It.) In moderate walking speed.

ANDANTINO—(It.) Modification of *andante*; whether faster or slower is not always clear.

BAR—The space between two bar-lines.

BAR-LINE—A vertical line on a staff dividing the staff into bars.

BASS CLEF—The F Clef. Locates F below Middle C.

BEAT—The rhythm to which you tap your foot. One beat = DOWN + UP.

CHORD—Two or more notes sounded together.

CLEF—A sign at the beginning of the staff indicating the names of the lines and spaces.

CODA—The "tail" or end of a piece of music. The composer's last word.

COMMON TIME—Time signature marked by the letter "C." Same as 4/4 time.

CRESCENDO—(It.) Gradually getting louder ($<$ or cresc.).

CUT TIME—Double the tempo (with half note as the beat). *Alla breve.*

DA CAPO—(It.) Repeat from the beginning (D.C.).

DA CAPO AL FINE—(It.) Repeat from the beginning to the end.

DAL SEGNO—(It.) Repeat from the sign (D.S.).

D.C.—(It.) Da Capo. Repeat from the beginning.

DECRESCENDO—(It.) Gradually getting softer ($>$ or decres.).

DIMINUENDO—(It.) Gradually getting softer ($>$ or dim.).

DOTS—A small dot after a note or rest adds half the note's value. A dot over or under a note means to play the note short.

DOUBLE BAR-LINE—Marks the end of the music or section.

D.S.—(It.) Dal Segno. Repeat from the sign.

D.S. AL CODA—(It.) Repeat from the sign to the Coda.

EIGHTH NOTE—An eighth of a whole note.

ENHARMONIC — Notes with different names that sound the same.

F CLEF—Bass clef. Tells location of F below Middle C.

FERMATA—(It.) Pause. Hold.

FINE—(It.) The End.

FLAT—Lowers a note.

FORTE—(It.) Loud (f).

FORTISSIMO—(It.) Very loud (ff).

FORTISSISSIMO—(It.) As loud as possible (fff).

G CLEF—Treble clef. Tells location of G above Middle C.

HALF NOTE—Half a whole note.

HOLD—Pause. *Fermata.*

KEY NOTE—Starting note of a scale.

KEY SIGNATURE—Group of sharps or flats right after the clef. Tells which notes are sharped or flatted in a song.

LARGHETTO—(It.) Rather slowly. Not as slow as *largo.*

LARGO—(It.) Slow, dignified tempo.

LEGATO—(It.) Smooth, connected.

LEGER LINES — Short lines written in when needed for notes above and below the staff.

LENTO—(It.) Slow.

LISTESSO TEMPO—(It.) The same speed.

LYRICS—The words to a song.

MAJOR SCALE—Scale starting on first note of a major key and proceeding up alphabetically by letter.

MEASURE—Same as bar.

MELODY—The tune.

METRONOME—A clock-like instrument that is used for setting tempo.

MEZZO—(It.) Half.

MEZZO-FORTE—(It.) Moderately loud (mf).

MEZZO-PIANO—(It.) Moderately soft (mp).

MIDDLE C—The note *C*, in the middle of the piano or keyboard.

MODERATO—(It.) Medium tempo.

MOLTO—(It.) Very.

NATURAL NOTE—A note that is not Sharp or Flat. A, B, C, D, E, F, G.

NATURAL SIGN—Placed in front of a note to cancel a sharp or flat.

NOTE — A musical sound or a sign that represents a musical sound.

OCTAVE—The span of all eight notes in a scale. From any note to the repeat of that note above it.

PHRASE—Similar to a line of poetry in language. Usually several measures long.

PIANISSIMO—(It.) Very soft (pp).

PIANISSISSIMO—(It.) As soft as possible (ppp).

PIANO—(It.) Soft (p).

PITCH—The height or depth of a sound. A specific musical tone.

PIU—(It.) More.

POCO—(It.) Little.

PRESTISSIMO—(It.) Very, very fast.

PRESTO—(It.) Very quickly.

QUARTER NOTE—A quarter of a whole note.

RALLENTANDO—(It.) Gradually slowing (rall.).

REPEATS—Means that the music is to be repeated. There are several kinds of repeat signs.

RESTS—Signs that indicate silence.

RITARDANDO—(It.) Gradually slowing (rit. or ritard.).

SCALE—A series of notes in alphabetical order, starting with the key note.

SHARP—Raises a note.

SIGNATURE—There are two signatures: time signature and key signature.

SIXTEENTH NOTE—One sixteenth of a whole note.

SLUR—A curved line that means the notes are to be played or sung smoothly.

SOLO—(It.) Alone; one player.

STACCATO—(It.) Detached. Space between notes.

STAFF—Five parallel lines and four spaces on which music is written.

SYNCOPATION—Off the beat. Music that starts on "up."

TEMPO—(It.) The speed of the music.

TIE—A curved line that connects notes and adds up their values.

TIME SIGNATURE—Two numbers at beginning of music. Top number tells how many beats in a measure; bottom number tells which kind of note gets a beat.

TREBLE CLEF—G clef locating G above Middle C on the staff.

TRIPLET—Three notes that fit into the time of two.

VIVACE—(It.) Quick, vivacious.

VIVO—(It.) Alive.

WHOLE NOTE—The longest note. Usually gets four beats.

APPENDIX B
MUSIC-RELATED ORGANIZATIONS

AMATEUR CHAMBER MUSIC PLAYERS, INC.
545 Eighth Avenue
New York, NY 10018

Organization of people who like to play or sing chamber music.

AMERICAN COLLEGE OF MUSICIANS,
NATIONAL GUILD OF PIANO TEACHERS
P.O. Box 1807
Austin, TX 78767

Promotes music education with an established standardized curriculum for piano teachers and students.

AMERICAN HARP SOCIETY, INC.
6331 Quebec Drive
Hollywood, CA 90068

Purpose is to cultivate, sponsor, and develop the appreciation of the harp as a musical instrument among its members and the general public.

AMERICAN MUSIC CENTER
30 W. 26th Street, Suite 1001
New York, NY 10010

Official United States information center for music.

AMERICAN MUSICAL INSTRUMENT SOCIETY
c/o The Shrine to Music Museum
414 East Clark
Vermillion, SD 57069

International organization founded to promote study of the history, design, and use of musical instruments in all cultures and from all historical periods.

AMERICAN ORFF-SCHULWERK ASSOCIATION
P.O. Box 391089
Cleveland, OH 44139

Maintains communication and cooperation among all Orff-Schulwerk-influenced music educators.

AMERICAN SCHOOL BAND DIRECTOR'S ASSOCIA-
TION
P.O. Box 146
Otsego, MI 49078

Dedicated to the advancement and improvement of instrumental music instruction in elementary and secondary
schools.

AMERICAN STRING TEACHERS ASSOCIATION
c/o Don Dillon Associates
4020 McEwen, Suite 105
Dallas, TX 75244

A musical and educational organization serving string (including guitar and harp) and orchestra teachers, players, and
students.

ASSOCIATION OF CONCERT BANDS OF AMERICA,
INC.
3020 Majestic Ridge
Las Cruces, NM 88001

Professional organization for adult band musicians, directors,
music educators, and band enthusiasts that promotes and
assists community/municipal and concert bands world-
wide.

ASSOCIATION OF PERFORMING ARTS PRESENTERS
1112 16th Street, N.W., Suite 620
Washington, DC 20036

Professional association for organizations involved in the pre-
sentation of the professional, touring performing arts.

CHAMBER MUSIC AMERICA
545 Eighth Avenue
New York, NY 10018

National service organization whose purpose is to advance the
interests of chamber music in all its forms.

CHRISTIAN INSTRUMENTAL DIRECTORS ASSOCIA-
TION
4826 Shabbona Road
Deckerville, MI 48427

Professional association to meet the needs of the church-related private school instrumental music directors and church musicians who use instrumental music in worship.

CONDUCTOR'S GUILD, INC.
P.O. Box 3361
West Chester, PA 19381

International organization open to all conductors of symphony orchestras, opera, ballet, choral ensembles, music theater, wind ensembles, bands, and similar groups.

INTERNATIONAL ASSOCIATION OF JAZZ EDUCA-TORS
Box 724
Manhattan, KS 66502

Nonprofit volunteer organization dedicated to fostering and promoting the understanding, appreciation, and artistic performance of jazz music in the schools.

INTERNATIONAL LEAGUE OF WOMEN COMPOSERS
S. Shore Road, Box 670, Pt. Peninsula
Three Mile Bay, NY 13693

Seeks to expand opportunities for women in composition.

INTERNATIONAL SOCIETY FOR MUSIC EDUCATION
14 Bedford Square
London, WCIB 3JC ENGLAND

Stimulates music education throughout the world as an integral part of general education and community life.

MUSIC DISTRIBUTOR'S ASSOCIATION
136 West 21st Street
New York, NY 10011

Made up of companies that manufacture, wholesale, or distribute musical merchandise to retail stores and manufacturers as well as importers who distribute through wholesalers.

MUSIC INDUSTRY CONFERENCE
c/o MENC
1902 Association Drive
Reston, VA 22091

Auxiliary of the Music Educators National Conference composed of suppliers of goods and services to the music education community.

NATIONAL ASSOCIATION OF BAND INSTRUMENT MANUFACTURERS
c/o Gemeinhardt Company
P.O. Box 788
Elkhart, IN 46515

Promotes the growth of instrumental music throughout the world.

NATIONAL ASSOCIATION OF COMPOSERS/USA
84 Cresta Verde Drive
Rolling Hills Estates, CA 90274

Performs, publishes, broadcasts, and houses contemporary music by American composers, and sponsors a composition contest and a contest for performers of new music.

NATIONAL MUSIC COUNCIL
45 W. 34th Street, #1010
New York, NY 10001

Provides a forum for professional, educational, industrial, and lay musical interests in the U.S.

NATIONAL PIANO FOUNDATION
4020 McEwen, Suite 105
Dallas, TX 75244

Organization of educators, technicians, retailers, and professional musicians that encourages the benefits and pleasures of playing piano, provides consumer information, and acts as a forum for communication between different branches of the piano industry network.

NATIONAL SCHOOL ORCHESTRA ASSOCIATION
39 East 200 South
Smithfield, UT 84335

Supports instrumental music teachers dedicated to the development of school orchestra programs.

ORGANIZATION OF AMERICAN KODALY EDUCATORS
Department of Music, Box 2017
Nicholls State University
Thibodaux, LA 70302

Maintains communication and cooperation among all Kodaly-influenced music educators.

SOCIETY FOR ETHNOMUSICOLOGY
Morrison Hall 005
Indiana University
Bloomington, IN 47408

Promotes the study of ethnic music.

THE SUZUKI ASSOCIATION OF THE AMERICAS, INC.
P.O. Box 354
Muscatine, IA 52761

Nonprofit organization of teachers, parents, and educators dedicated to implementing the Suzuki Method in North America.

INDEX